VOICELESS WHISPERS

Tuning Into Nature's Messages

M.J. Domet

BALBOA.
PRESS

A DIVISION OF HAY HOUSE

Balboa Press books may be ordered through booksellers or by contacting:

Balboa Press
A Division of Hay House
1663 Liberty Drive
Bloomington, IN 47403
www.balboapress.com
1 (877) 407-4847

Because of the dynamic nature of the Internet, any web addresses or links contained in this book may have changed since publication and may no longer be valid. The views expressed in this work are solely those of the author and do not necessarily reflect the views of the publisher, and the publisher hereby disclaims any responsibility for them.

The author of this book does not dispense medical advice or prescribe the use of any technique as a form of treatment for physical, emotional, or medical problems without the advice of a physician, either directly or indirectly. The intent of the author is only to offer information of a general nature to help you in your quest for emotional and spiritual well-being. In the event you use any of the information in this book for yourself, which is your constitutional right, the author and the publisher assume no responsibility for your actions.

Any people depicted in stock imagery provided by Thinkstock are models, and such images are being used for illustrative purposes only.
Certain stock imagery © Thinkstock.

Printed in the United States of America.

ISBN: 978-1-5043-2505-9 (sc)
ISBN: 978-1-5043-2507-3 (hc)
ISBN: 978-1-5043-2506-6 (e)

Library of Congress Control Number: 2014921910

Balboa Press rev. date: 2/5/2015

To all the animals in my life: those I have known and loved and also those who have impacted my life in some way, however small, but always with the intent of sharing profound knowledge with me.

Lots of people talk to animals …
Not very many listen, though.
That's the problem.
—Benjamin Hoff

The purity of a person's heart can be quickly
measured by how they regard animals.
—Unknown

CONTENTS

INTRODUCTION

I have always had animals in my life. I can remember living on the farm near Valhalla Centre, Alberta, when I was just a toddler and being surrounded by dogs, cats, chickens, cows, and horses. I am pretty sure there were a few mice around as well. I can recall my dad finding a mouse nest and those tiny pink babies, resembling shrimp, squirming on the ground. At that time, I didn't realize there were special energy meanings associated with the animals—they were just family (well, most of them!) Of course, there were a few pets that were so special I can recall their names to this day. There was Ring, a black collie dog with a white ring around his neck. Ring was trained to pull me and my sisters around on a sled in the winter. We all loved that dog!

Then there was Clucky—my own special hen. She was my constant companion, as I was the oldest child, and my sisters were too small to be any fun. Clucky and I were the best of friends. We spent a good deal of our time swinging on a home fashioned swing in the barn, and she followed me all around the yard whenever I was outside. That is—whenever she wasn't being packed in my arms. I can still remember how slighted I felt when Clucky became a mother. I had been looking all over for her for days, and she was nowhere to be seen. Finally, Dad found her outside beside a huge boulder just on the edge of the hayfield. I was so excited to know she was okay and thought she would be just as happy to see me. My heart broke when she nipped my fingers as I reached across her newly-hatched chicks to pet her. We did make up, but somehow it was never the same.

I won't ever forget the horses—King and Queen. They were large working horses, but—oh—how I loved them! I learned to ride when I was four or five years old, and it is something that I still love to do. For quite a few years, once we moved to town and other interests gained my attention, I didn't ride much. It wasn't until we moved to the farm where I now reside that horseback riding became a passion again. The first thing we bought for our new farm was a riding horse, and I have had from one to five of them here at various times since then.

Of course, we moved to the country with a dog and a cat and have had up to four dogs and countless cats at any one time. We also have numerous birds and wildlife and the occasional visit from the neighbors' animals. Right now, we are also blessed with a snake and fish who live with us.

Although I have always loved animals of any kind, the energetic meanings associated with them weren't evident to me until I began working with energy modalities and strengthening my relationship to life of all forms.

When Reiki[1] became a part of my existence several years ago, my concept of life changed, and I realized the sacredness of connection to all. While giving Reiki treatments, I began receiving messages from animals for my clients, which were in alignment with the clients' experiences at the time. During this period, I also received the information from a very wise friend that my totem animal was a raven. Something about this information resonated deep within my core, and when I read about the meaning of raven medicine in Ted Andrews' book, *Animal Speak*,[2] I had to laugh. The part about hoarding and being a tease about it was so right on. I remember, while growing up, I used to hold on to all my Easter candy while my sisters gobbled theirs right up. I would then take mine out and eat it slowly and tantalizingly while they watched, empty handed, because their treats were all gone. This only worked for so long until my parents realized what was happening, and then I had to share my sweets with my siblings.

---

[1]   A gentle energy modality that releases unwanted blocks within the physical, emotional, and spiritual body.

[2]   Llewellyn 1993

Many other traits of the raven resonated with me, while some were, as I was to find out, a vision of things to come. At that time, I didn't see myself as a spiritual healer or animal communicator at all.

As I progressed along my spiritual path and healed from many of my experiences as I have recalled in my first book, the multi-award winning memoir, *Waves of Blue Light: Heal the Heart and Free the Soul*,[3] I found myself opening up more and more to the energy of the animals attempting to channel through me. I began to give readings using Steven Farmer's amazing *Messages from Your Animal Spirit Guides* card decks[4] and found that I was able to also *see* or perceive the animal totem or spirit guide of the person sitting across from me. The response of clients when their guide reveals itself is very positive and reaffirming. A few people who may have their heart set on a supposed romantic or strong animal as a totem, and find out it is not as they expected, are usually quickly satisfied once the traits of their particular guide are revealed. All animal energies from the ant to the zebra, and everyone in between, are strong, positive, and revealing of the character of their human counterpart. None are to be dismissed as weak or nonessential, just as no human is more relevant than another. The sense of power we often tend to exhibit over our animal friends is a result of our own limited thinking and distorted view of the world.

It is interesting to note, as well, that every workshop I teach has its own spirit animal guide coming in to help.[5] Once identified, it is amazing how much each person in that particular class relates to the characteristics of the animal that reveals itself.

Within the pages of this book are stories that have come from the heart of the experiences of the authors. I hope you will laugh with them, cry with them, and above all, fall in love with the creatures that have made

---

[3]   Xlibris, 2011

[4]   Hay House, 2008

[5]   Visit www.expecttobeempowered.com to view a list of workshops.

a difference in their lives and in the lives of others. I have kept the stories as authentic as possible, only making the occasional change to capture the flow of the tale. You will notice the various styles of writing and get a sense of the individual personality of each author as you read their story. Thank you from the bottom of my heart to all the fabulous story and image authors who have contributed to the making of this book!

And, whenever you encounter any one of our animal kingdom friends, remember how very special you must be to warrant their time and attention, so they can deliver the messages you need to hear.

Are you listening?

There are several books you can access in order to interpret any messages from nature's animal kingdom. Here are a few of our favorites:

Animal Spirit Guides by Steven Farmer, Published by Hay House

Animal Speak by Ted Andrews, Published by Llewellyn

Animal Activities by Narayan Singh, Published by Lynne R Henderson Publications

I am available at expecttobeempowered@gmail.com if you are interested in having an Animal Spirit Guide Reading and Channeling.

Please visit my website at www.expecttobeempowered.com for a free download of Twelve Enlightening Ways to Live an Empowered Life and other inspirational messages.

Blessings for an enriched life filled with meaningful connections.

—M. J.

EMBRACING THE CONNECTION

Affirmation: My body, mind, and soul connect with the divine essence of nature, empowering me with knowledge beyond the five senses.

Voiceless Whispers

Whispering wings beat when it is quiet—
A definite hush precedes the relayed message,
Fearful that noise will disguise communication so freely sent.
The receiver's occupied mind, so immersed in his daily routine,
Misses the opportunity that reaches for his attention.

Silent feet pad along with just a glimpse of
the furred body housing the soul—
The desire to relay a message only ignored by virtue of a day rushed.
Moving in a circle of trust, hoping to make contact,
The crier's profound message unnoticed
as thoughts are lost in a focus,
Not ending at the sun's demise, but rising up again with a new day.

Whispering wings beat when it is quiet—
A definite hush precedes the relayed message,
Fearful that noise will disguise communication so freely sent.
The receiver's occupied mind, so immersed in his daily routine,
Misses the opportunity that reaches for his attention.

Insects crawl through the grainy soil; cross the path of the unwary—
Slipping in and out of the way of booted feet
intent on making their destination,
Hoping to be noticed before being trampled beneath rubbery soles—
Unsuccessful, as urgent matters are at hand,
and there is no time to slow down.
Crushed and broken, the message lost in the
ensuing burden of fighting time.

Whispering wings beat when it is quiet—
A definite hush precedes the relayed message,
Fearful that noise will disguise communication so freely sent.
The receiver's occupied mind, so immersed in his daily routine,
Misses the opportunity that reaches for his attention.

Sea life wavering through endless waves of
cold, determined to beat them—
Fighting the weeds, manmade pollution, and endless lines of plastic
To carry on tradition and unyielding demands
to mark the distance yet to go—
Pausing to let man know what life burdens he need not carry.
Communication halted as, once again, message trounced.

Whispering wings beat when it is quiet—
A definite hush precedes the relayed message,
Fearful that noise will disguise communication so freely sent.
The receiver's occupied mind, so immersed in his daily routine,
Misses the opportunity that reaches for his attention.

Will we slow and stop to listen to the voiceless whispers
That come our way?
An attempt at communication that is unheard,
Lost in the sounds of a rushed life.
Pain, fear, and anguish can be uncovered by the messages
If we choose to hear whispering wings, silent feet, crawling,
Slithering bodies of nature's messengers
And realize their sacrifices allow them to align
With the souls of angels.

Natural Empowerment

To me, there is nothing more peaceful or empowering than being in the gentle, balanced energy of nature. Whether it is walking through the trees with the sun sending sparkles of light filtering through the green, upturned leaves on a beautiful summer day, or with the cold of winter seeping through my many layers of clothing and my lined boots, which are alternating between the crunch-and-squeak rhythm of walking through the snow, I feel at home. Adding to the joyous barking of my dogs as they scramble through the trees, chasing their real or imagined nemeses, and hearing the seemingly orchestrated high, low, and somewhere in-between pitches of birds singing and the sudden scampering of small animals in the underbrush, I recognize the connected oneness of nature's heartbeat and that of my own. I see nature as something not to be conquered or controlled but accepted as a piece of myself to be loved unconditionally and enjoyed for what it is.

Attuning to the rhythm of nature's voice brings us closer to hearing her cries of pain when she is forced to give up a piece of herself and also to her cries of joy when she is heard and understood. The greatest challenge is to understand that the natural world is not separate from humankind; it is the part of us that recognizes ourselves. The sun rises each morning and sets each evening as we do. We—and nature—have our gloomy days when we need to be introspective and our sunny days when we are outgoing and fun-loving. Nature—like us—has a time for rebirth, a time to grow, and a time to die.

Mother Nature also shows us the give-and-take of destruction and devastation. We take from her, and she balances out this act. Our thoughts are evident to the universe. When we become overburdened with the cares and worries of our daily lives and feel overwhelmed, beat ourselves up, and judge others, nature becomes our jury and shows us through her powerful being how our thoughts and actions are destroying us.

The power of our relationship with our natural surroundings is strong, and the birds, animals, fish, and insects that share this beautiful space with us have our best interests at heart. They continuously communicate with us through their presence and actions. Depending on the animal, we can react with fear, annoyance, or ignorance, or we can take the time to hear and understand their celestial message.

If a creature appears and reappears continuously, most people tend to associate its presence to something physical, such as available food, and not look much deeper than that. Upon recognizing there is something more to look for, it becomes evident that, again, nature is showing us another way to connect and communicate.

Animals, whether they are wild or tame, have an energy that is closely related to that of ours. Each species has its own characteristics, strengths, and weaknesses. When there is an unusual or repetitive visitation by a certain animal, it wants your attention in order to deliver a message to you. It could be a communication from your favorite deceased pet or a message asking you to be aware of something presently going on in your life. Your attentiveness to these messages can bring you peace. Once a situation is revealed to you, you are able to deal with it before it becomes more difficult. You also learn to appreciate awareness of something greater going on in your life than you may have been previously conscious of. The stories in this book will give insight into many different situations involving animals. You will become aware of the timing and interpretation each of the authors display as they tell their stories of tuning into nature's messages.

Messages are very rarely given to anyone served on a silver platter in a clear, connect-the-dot pattern. They are, however, delivered in a way that leaves no doubt to the receiver of the message as to the meaning of the communication.

Although many of the stories in this book could be placed into more than one category, I have intuitively chosen to interpret the experiences according to their strongest message. All of the domestic animals could be placed in the companion section—but often the delivery of a lesson or further connection warrants placement within a category that is not as obvious.

The love of animals is evident in each of these stories, and the connection between our furred, feathered, and finned friends and us human animals is strong and sound. It is apparent that we are all here to teach and learn from one another.

I know some amazing people. It is inspiring to have such a great group of teachers around me. I hear a variety of stories from my students, especially in Reiki classes, as we discuss the five principles of Reiki. One of these principles is to *honor every living thing*. Awareness of this concept often brings up stories of connection with animals.

Following are two examples of the many tales I hear whenever animals come up as a subject:

Ladybug Magic

One of my students, Denise, adopted a ladybug for the winter. She had found it in her house and gave it food and water for a few months, as it was too cold to put it outside. She didn't keep it in a jar or locked up anywhere. It was allowed to make its own choices and come and go as it pleased.

She didn't have to do this and many wouldn't have been bothered, thinking it was just a bug, but Denise's heart is big. To honor the ladybug's life when she found it had died, she gently laid it to rest in one of her plants.

—As told by **Denise Kendall,** *who grew up on Cape Breton Island, Nova Scotia, but now lives in Grande Prairie, Alberta. She has been blessed with a beautiful singing voice as well as a beautiful heart.*

A ladybug in your life is magical. It offers protection from the opinions of others and often comes around when you are moving forward spiritually—which is exactly what was going on in Denise's life at that time. When she no longer needed it, the ladybug moved on.

In one of my animal spirit guide classes, a student told me this amazing story of an incident that happened on a family trip. Her family was coming back from the funeral of a young relative who had been hit by a car while crossing a city street. In their grief, they maintained that, without a doubt, the accident could have been avoided. While discussing the seeming impossibility of not being able to see someone crossing the street, a moose appeared on the road right in front of them, and the driver had to swerve into the ditch to avoid hitting the animal.

Was that a message? They sure thought so!

We receive messages from nature every day, but it is our lack of attention and knowledge that prevents us from making the connection between what is going on in our world and how it affects everything around us.

Once we begin to see the interrelationship between our planet and every living thing on it and ourselves, things change. Our awareness brings a new perception and an ability to see things differently, creating a long-lasting, mutually beneficial energetic correspondence with all.

May you always be blessed with voiceless whispers!

ANIMALS AS COMPANIONS

Affirmation: When I embrace the energies of my animal companions, my body, mind, and soul accept and understand unconditional love.

In and Out of Trees

He came into my life one warm fall day;
From a litter of nine, he was the one to stay
By my side—for twelve years and a bit.

Each day through those years he greeted me,
His love and loyalty easy to see
Through his life—right to the end.

From puppyhood on, he seemed all smiles.
Each time we saddled the horses and rode for miles,
In and out of trees—he followed along.

He greeted all much the same way
By raising his paws; he was asking to play.
No matter who or when—no opportunity missed.

Age, I saw, slowly took him away;
But in his eyes, come what may,
Was always that spark—his light.

One night the light left his eyes;
And as the dog I loved said his good-byes,
My heart felt heavy—in so much pain.

There is one thing I know without a doubt;
Somewhere up there, he's running about,
In and out of trees—loving me still.

THE ANIMAL PARTNER

Probably the best known connection humankind has with the animal kingdom is that of a companion. Our animal companions often become beloved members of our family. For some people, they are a confidante, playmate, and protector all in one. It can be as difficult to lose a pet as it is to lose a family member.

As a companion, our pets play a more important role on a spiritual level than we often realize. Since they have come into our lives for direct contact, or a long-term commitment, their job comes with a varied description.

They may be helping their owner release past life karma such as negative or abusive behavior toward animals or this particular animal. If this animal has chosen to come into this lifetime with you and tends to adopt you as their owner over others in the family, it is your karma that is being recognized. With no designated favorite, the entire family may be cohesively balancing out a situation.

Another role of the companion animal could be in assisting you with communication, as it may be easier for you to tell your feelings, hopes, and dreams to someone who will listen unconditionally, without a fear of being judged. It may also help you with opening up to love, if this has been an issue in your life.

Sometimes pets take on an individual's emotional or physical issue, choosing to do this because of their love for you or because you aren't able to handle things on your own. Quite possibly, they have chosen to be your mirror and make the invisible visible to you.

Whatever role your pet has chosen to play in your life, they do it with unconditional love and deserve to be honored and respected. It is all too easy to take your animal friends for granted.

Because so many of us become attached to our pets, it can be difficult to let them go when it is their time to leave, either in death, re-ownership, or loss in any way. Your pet knows when they have served the purpose they have come here for. I know this does not make it any easier for you to let them go, but be assured they are still looking out for you from wherever they are. Just as you move on from one job to another or from one relationship to another, they need to move on as well—once their purpose has been served in a particular area.

Dogs

I have had many animal companions in my life, mainly in the form of dogs, cats, and horses, and more recently—a snake. Some of these animals have left my life in ordinary ways—through death or gone missing, but there are two incidents, about two very special dogs, I am going to share with you that have been very different.

Personally, I don't think any animal has more personality than a dog. Dogs teach us how to be human. Generally, they are warm, loving, and loyal, no matter how they have been shunned or treated by their owner. Each day is a new beginning, and all is forgiven when the sun rises. Whether you have been gone five minutes or five days, you are greeted as if you have been gone for five years. Who doesn't love to be missed like that!

Our loyal companions, dogs, tend to be devoted to those they love. They will never abandon or betray their owners and will set aside their own needs to ensure the safety and happiness of those they are here to help and protect. They form strong attachments and will put themselves in the path of danger if they think their loved ones are in trouble. Along with their sense of duty, dogs bring us innocence, strength, courage, and an insatiable urge to play. In fact, other than being dependent upon us for food, playing with them is all they tend to ask for.

A sociable animal, dogs love the companionship of other animals or people. They have a strong sense of fairness and immediate intuitive knowledge whether or not someone is to be trusted.

Dogs tend to be the most sought-after pet of any other animal because of their ability to socialize and display unconditional love. By observing their behavior, we are able to learn social skills and methods of interacting with others in a way that brings ourselves and others joy.

How do you greet the people in your life?

Do you embrace life with a sense of innocence and playfulness?

Do you forgive readily?

Do you socialize easily and form strong attachments?

Do you stand up for yourself and others?

Are your boundaries clear?

The first story I want to relate to you is about Clyde, who was with me for over twelve years and is the inspiration for the poem, "In and Out of Trees," at the beginning of this chapter.

Clyde was born on our farm to our German shepherd–collie dog, Bonnie, as a result of her liaison with a Great Pyrenees wanderer, who was making his rounds across the countryside leaving a trail of many look-alike puppies. He left nine of his offspring in this particular litter with us.

Originally, Clyde, as a six-week-old puppy, left us to go live with a family in the city, but he repeatedly dug under their fence and freed himself from his backyard prison to run around town creating havoc.

So, we got him back. He was always the sweetest dog and playfully wrestled with his sister, Cleo, who we had kept from the litter until she was hit and killed by a vehicle about three years later. From then on, Clyde's canine companion and playmate was his mother, Bonnie, until she passed, and a succession of horses we added and subtracted to and from our pasture over the years.

Clyde was exceptionally smart and regularly performed for people when he wanted attention by sitting up on his hind legs and begging for a handshake. As Clyde took after his Pyrenees father in looks—he was a large, off-white dog—people were always amazed that this huge dog could actually sit on his haunches. Needless to say, he got people's attention. He was never happier than when he could be with his human companions, and it didn't matter who they were. Friends, family, strangers, adults, or children—Clyde was in his glory when people were around. We could trust Clyde with anyone from elderly people to small children, and he always honored that trust. People loved him as much as he loved them.

His second favorite thing was coming along when we went out riding on the horses. He bounded in and out of the bush with his tongue hanging out of his mouth and a big doggie smile plastered on his face.

When Clyde was about nine years old, he was hit by a vehicle on the road past our farm and dislocated his right shoulder. It didn't seem to bother him too much at the time, but as he got older we could see he was in some pain at times. Throughout it all, he remained Clyde and was as loveable as always—although we could see the age in his movements, and his hearing seemed diminished—but he never lost his enthusiasm for horseback riding, even though he had slowed down considerably. We knew it was inevitable that he would leave us sooner or later, but didn't really want to face it.

Late last spring, as my son's girlfriend was leaving for work, Clyde attacked her. He bit her right forearm right through to the bone and wouldn't let go. When she attempted to pry his mouth off of her arm with her other hand, he grabbed onto her fingers and bit hard. When she told me this, as I was driving her to emergency to get stitched up, I knew this was not a random act—it was deliberate. She also was not a stranger. Having lived with my son for the past few months, she had interacted with Clyde every day—often several times a day.

It broke my heart to know that we had to put him down, but we could not have an unpredictable dog around. Clyde was thirteen years old. What led to this unusual act of violence?

I have two theories. The first one is that we weren't letting him go energetically, so he forced our hand. The second is that he was trying to tell us about our son's relationship. You see, our son had just announced his engagement to his girlfriend a few weeks before. About a month after we put Clyde down, the girlfriend left with the new car our son had just bought her. There were a few other things we learned later, which could have added some difficulty to the relationship, had it progressed into marriage. What do you think? Was Clyde trying to give us one last gift?

My second story is about a puppy that brought so much joy to my life. I named him Denziel, and no—he was not black. It seems as though people thought I named him after Denzel Washington (whom I absolutely love as an actor), but his name was born out of a game my granddaughter and I played when picking up our puppies from a friend a few years back.

At that time we had two dogs, Apollo and Clyde, having recently lost Bonnie. We used to call them A, B, and C for short. So, it was jokingly that I told Alexis, my granddaughter, that we needed to choose names, one beginning with B and one that started with D in order to once again have A, B, C, and then an added D. She almost immediately named her pup Beckie, and I was struggling with finding an appropriate name for my wiggling, playful, golden brown ball of fur. At some point the name, Denziel, came to my mind, and I thought it appropriately unusual enough for this beautiful mutt with so much personality.

Denziel and I became fast friends and companions. I spoilt him badly by letting him sit on my knee, even when he grew too big to fit comfortably.

He was terribly jealous of the other dogs if they came near me and would growl and bare his teeth at them until they backed away. I tried to discipline him for his bad behavior, but wasn't successful a lot of the time. I didn't think he would actually fight with the other dogs, but he did start something once in a while that I had to break up. He was also aggressive with food (I know—you are thinking about the raven connection, aren't you?), and the other three dogs just had to wait their turns while he gulped down the juiciest morsels unless I stepped in.

Denziel was just over a year old when I came back from town one day and saw him lying on the road just off of our driveway. We used to live on a fairly quiet rural road, but it had become quite busy in the last few years with oilfield traffic. Anyway, when I first noticed something lying there, I thought it was a coyote because Denziel was close to the same color. But … then I saw the tail. It had black streaks woven through the brown and white strands of hair. It was then that I knew it was Denziel, and he didn't seem to be moving. I know I stopped the car, but that is all I remember clearly.

I was heartbroken. I had given my love to this tough little mutt and watched him grow throughout the last year only to find him out here on the road, still and unmoving. Living on a farm, I have had to say good-bye to many animals, but some were harder to let go of than others. Denziel was one of these.

Another year passed and my son and his girlfriend brought home a tiny little ball of golden fluff that they named Bailey. Bailey is a golden retriever and, at first, I just thought of her as another dog and not one that I saw too often as her owners lived on our property but not with us. It wasn't until Bailey was a few months old that I noticed the coloring similarities to Denziel—minus the black tail hair.

As summer came around, Bailey spent more and more time outside with my three dogs. I was thinking how much she was beginning to act like Denziel with her aggressive jealous behavior (which I have been told is unusual conduct in this breed of dog) but didn't voice these thoughts aloud. I think I was afraid of getting too close again and, besides, she wasn't really my dog, even though she spent most of her time on my deck. It was my granddaughter who verbalized what I had been thinking when she said to me one day, "Grandma, doesn't Bailey remind you of Denziel?" I think I replied noncommittedly, "Maybe a little."

It was early fall when my son and his girlfriend split up, and when she took Bailey with her, my immediate thought was that I must have been wrong about believing that Bailey and Denziel were one and the same.

About two weeks later, Bailey was back on my deck. I asked my son about it, and he said that they were sharing Bailey—like a joint custody arrangement. *Oh*, I thought, *maybe I am not wrong about this after all.*

Well, Bailey has disappeared and reappeared many different times. Even though she is supposed to be staying with David on his week, she often seems to be around my house and is always the first one to ask for a treat—as well as first to the food dish—aggressively keeping the other dogs at bay until she eats her fill. Lately, Bailey is a more permanent fixture here as her *mom* lives in town and doesn't have the room for this growing dog to run around free like we do here on the farm.

So far, I have kept my distance—but time will tell. If it looks as if Bailey is sticking around permanently, I may have to get down, look her in the eye, and welcome her home.

It is possible that Denziel left too soon, before we had a chance to complete whatever it is that is our destiny together in this lifetime. He may not have been able to work as efficiently with me in spirit form and so chose to come back to see this contract through to completion. It is also possible that he has a double purpose with his *real family* and came back this way in order to work with all of us.

Oh—and one more thing! David and his girlfriend had never planned on getting a dog. They happened to stop in to visit an old friend of David's while on a 4-wheeling trip. This friend was at home waiting for someone to pick up his last puppy. His contact didn't show up at the appointed time and hadn't shown up when they were ready to leave, so Bailey, who by that time had captured both of their hearts, came home with them.

Coincidence or timing? Maybe a little of both!

Continuing on with the theme of dogs as companion animals, this next story will warm your heart as a connection between human and dog is evident as a bond so strong as to be unbreakable is revealed. The author of this story, Don Shine, is eighty-eight years old and has never forgotten his loving companion, Coco.

A Boy and His Dog

While walking in the early evening breeze wafting in from the Pacific Ocean, as I was wont to do, I came upon a boy sitting on a log born of a previous raging sea that was giving him a perch. As he sat gazing into the future, his dog sat beside him, bringing solace to the tortured soul of one so recently abandoned by his family of birth.

Thinking that it was best not to interfere with a brokenhearted boy with a tear running down his face, I sat down nearby and muttered a prayer of compassion toward him and watched as his dog sat there beside him licking away the tears.

The light of day was fading as the boy arose. Seeing me sitting some small distance away, he gingerly approached. "Please, mister, do not think badly of me," he said, "but I have not eaten in three days." Thinking he must have noticed my lunch bag at my side, I offered him a sandwich and a drink. The first thing he did was break off a morsel of food and give it to his dog, who waved his tail gratefully. The boy then sat beside me devouring the sandwich.

The three of us sat silently together for a while, and then I asked, "Do you and your dog have shelter for the night?" Shortly after he had sorrowfully explained his plight of being homeless, the boy found himself tucked into a warm, cozy bed with his dog—a wary look in his eye—lying beside him.

The light of the coal oil lamp dimmed as the eyes of the boy and his dog closed peacefully into the night, to be awakened by a glorious ray of sunshine thrust into the room the following morning. Groggily, the boy and his dog awoke to the smell of bacon and eggs wafting through the room and soon found themselves devouring the savory meal with a mug of cocoa to wash it down.

The boy grew into a fine young man wearing the uniform of a member of the Royal Canadian Air Force during the Second World War, his dog, Coco, a stray who had joined him on the beach that fateful day, by his side.

The love between a boy and a stray dog on the beach touched my heart, an experience I shall never forget, as I was that boy lost so many years ago. Growing old with the memory of my dog named Coco lifting my spirit, a tear drops from my chin as I kneel and say a prayer while pinning a bright red poppy upon the cross of his grave.

This man of many years of age carries the love of his dog from long ago. This love gives him the strength to carry on until the dog, Coco, and the man are reunited, once again sitting on a log together by the sea and munching on a bite of food so freely given by a stranger.

—**Don Shine** *(White Raven)—Bio by Charles Bidwell*

He is unsinkable. He has survived situations where many would have thrown in the towel. He sticks with his friends through depression and dis-ease and gave one the gift of surgery to regain clear sight. He is an internal seeker—reading voraciously and widely, especially in the area of spirit and both physical and mental health. He believes that each person shares responsibility for his own health in consultation with professionally trained healers. He insists on being informed of what is going on in his body and what steps he can take to reinforce the curative measures that are prescribed. He goes beyond western medical science and explores alternative practices in an effort to live as long and healthily as possible. He caves in to acquire clothes, books, and furnishings. He yields easily to the impulse to purchase whatever will add to his comfort or well-being and often finds himself buried in an excess of things. Then he generously gives some of the surplus away. He has a playful nature and dresses as the mood strikes him. He writes poetry when the muse strikes to express a feeling or insight with impact. He is a very unique man.

The Cat

Cats, as well as dogs, have a reputation for being a companion animal, but as you will read farther on in this book, they are incredible teachers and connectors as well.

No animal seems to have more mysterious qualities than the cat. It can move from charming to vicious within seconds. Very unpredictable, the cat's self-absorbed, introverted, introspective manner often fools us as to what their intentions are from one minute to the next.

When in the mood, cats love to be stroked and petted and are very loving and calming. However, their independence will tell you when they have had enough, and they will move away from you and expect you to respect their fickle moods. As they listen to their own inner guidance, they expect you to do the same.

Often associated with the lore of witches, cats have a mystery about them. Their intuitiveness allows them to feel the energy and tune in to the emotions of other animals and humans. This is part of their magic. One day they may be loving and gracious and on another day may hide from you or angrily hiss at you.

Cats are the divas of the animal world. Their gracefulness, sensuality, and sophisticated appearance often hide a deeper, less charming personality. They expect to be treated regally and bring charm, personality, and often a look of luxury to the home, of which they are very protective.

Their nocturnal wanderings are part of the conflicting personality they exude, as night brings another side of this animal to the forefront. Very at home in the dark, house and feral cats alike pursue illicit pleasures at night where independent personalities may clash in a flurry of claws, teeth, and tails. It is all a part of the life of these creative, regal, clever creatures who continue to bewitch and charm us as they dream their epic tales of adventures while languishing sleepily in the afternoon sun.

What have your interactions with cats taught you?

Do you take enough risks? Or too many?

Are you confusing people by being charming and witty one minute and turning on them the next?

Are you too independent or not independent enough?

Are you tuning in to your intuition?

Do you respect the feelings of others?

Do you take the time to be introspective and find deeper meaning in your life?

While reading the following stories, you will see how having a cat for a companion has brought joy and happiness as well as unanticipated experiences into the lives of their owners.

The first story, "Ginger," shows how the connection between human and animal can be so strong that our intuition often takes precedence over logic.

In the second story, "Ole Blue Eyes," the author relates her experiences with a much loved, precocious cat whose adventures rival those of the famous Garfield.

GINGER

Ginger, a small, light, orange tabby cat, came into my life about eight months ago. When I met Ginger, she was a seven-month-old rescue cat rehabilitated by the local college's Animal Health Technology students. I was working for the college at the time. Unfortunately a number of jobs, including mine, were cut shortly after this, and I was suddenly at home all day trying to redefine my new role. Ginger was a big help during this transition. Sometimes she was the only one I talked to all day. And what a great listener! Sitting on my lap, purring, she gave me unconditional love and undivided attention. My husband, who is more of a dog person, even came to enjoy her company. Ginger fit right into our home.

Unfortunately, one night about three months ago, she didn't come home. Ginger was used to going in and out of the house and always came when I called her. I don't know how many times that first night I went to the back door and called her name. We went around the neighborhood asking people if they'd seen her and asked them to check their sheds. We put posters up and checked with the local rescue. I both walked and drove around looking for her. There was not one sign of her. One neighbor (I am sure she was trying to be helpful) told me that she'd seen foxes and that often they hunt cats—more so than coyotes, which are also around.

Three weeks had passed since I'd last seen Ginger. My husband mentioned a couple of times that maybe I should think about giving her things away, or at least put her food dish away. I wasn't ready, though. When I sat on the couch in the evenings, I could see her turning on her back, purring, and looking up at me like I was her favorite person, which I was! Her presence seemed so real that I just couldn't imagine she was gone, although I was starting to think I'd have to face that sad reality.

The morning after Thanksgiving I was roused from sleep by my husband's voice hollering, "Cheryl, you've got see who's here!" Stumbling into the kitchen, I was amazed and thrilled to see Ginger. I couldn't believe she was back! Her three-and-a-half-week adventure left her about three pounds lighter and with a bad wound on her left haunch and a lesser mark in the middle of her back. The vet said it looked like a bite mark, and maybe she'd run so far she'd gotten lost or gone into hiding. I wish she could tell me her story.

Ginger has been home a month now and gained back two pounds. She is happy and back to her old self—a bouncy, playful, ball of purr!

She is an inside cat only, now.

—**Cheryl Frank** *is of Dunne-za, Cree, and European descent; she has always felt an affinity with animals. Her parents taught her to respect and care for animals, and she continues to honor this. Cheryl shares her home with her husband of twenty-eight years, Eugene, and her cat Ginger. She has two grown sons, Travis and Troy.*

OLE BLUE EYES

I had decided I was buying a kitten for my daughter's birthday.

We headed out of town, and even though it was the day that a couple of tornadoes touched down in our home city, Grande Prairie, Alberta, nothing was keeping me from getting this Himalayan/Siamese kitten from Debolt, a small hamlet thirty minutes away. They only had one male kitten left. He was kind of scraggly, but we paid the fifty dollars they were asking for him and brought him home.

We named him Sammy, but often called him *Ole Blue Eyes* after Frank Sinatra, because of his dark blue eyes. He was truly one of a kind.

Soon after bringing Sammy home, I began finding this old Yeti doll in the living room, and when I asked the kids, they kept saying it wasn't them that put it there. Then my bras began showing up in the living room too! One day I came home early and found Sammy dragging the Yeti doll down the stairs and one of my bras lying on the stairs. I had to keep my bras down deep in the hamper from then on.

Sammy was not allowed outside at first because, at that time, there was someone poisoning cats where we lived. When he got older, I decided he needed to be outside—at least for a while. After trying out a few collars and long leashes, we had his routine down pat. He got to go out for a couple of hours a day.

One night he got loose when the chain broke. I called out for him, but he didn't come, so I settled in for the night. In the morning he still wasn't around, so I headed to work and came home to check on him at lunchtime. I called out his name and heard a faint meow coming from the back of the house where he was tangled up on the fence and in some trees. He was grounded for a couple of days until I got him a new leash.

A big tom cat started coming around to check Sammy out. I would check once in a while to see what was happening. A fight eventually broke out. My son, Jon, was there, and he chased the other cat away. He brought Sammy in, and I said, "That's not Sammy!" and he replied, "Yes, it is!" I didn't believe him, but he said when a cat gets scared, he fluffs out. I still didn't believe him—but it was true. If Jon hadn't been there, I would have chased Sammy off.

From the beginning, Sammy always came and slept with me. After a couple of weeks of having to constantly let him out of my room, I put a sock on my door so he could open the door himself—which he did. I should have shown him how to close it too!

We moved around quite a bit until I finally bought a house. In one of our rentals, there were some earthbound spirits. I had purposely chosen to live in this unit because I had had an encounter when I stayed in it before. I remember it clearly.

One night after going to bed, just before I fell asleep, I suddenly felt as if all the air was being sucked out of the room. Not knowing what else to do, I covered my head with my blanket and soon felt the bed begin to shake. When the bed shook a second time, I thought it was done, but when I went to uncover my head, the bed shook one more time. After what seemed like seconds, I again peeked and felt the air sweeping back into the room. I then knew it was done. I always slept with the light on after that. As other people had had similar experiences while living here, it was thought that the building might have been built on a vortex.

After living there for a few months, Sammy and I had just gotten into bed and were getting comfortable. All of a sudden, what felt like a big, round, six-inch metal ball landed at the foot of our bed. We both looked where it had bounced and didn't see anything, so we just went to sleep. Sammy always slept in front of me. If I moved to face the right, he would get up and face the right and vice versa. Maybe he was protecting and keeping me safe from other beings.

There were times I would leave him for a couple of days; I had those big refill food and water containers for him. One of those times was when I took my son with me to Edmonton to visit, and I was supposed to take him back to his dad's before heading home. The urge to go home first and check on Sammy was overpowering, so that's what I decided to do. When I got into the house, he didn't come to the door to greet me, so I started to call for him. I heard a faint meow and ran upstairs. He was stuck in a drawer in the captain's bed that I had told my daughter to make sure was always closed, because I was afraid of this very thing happening. I took his face and touched our foreheads together as I did every time I came home. I would do this for a couple of minutes to let him know I loved him.

On our last move together, one of my older daughters said that if I wanted to see my grandson, I would have to get rid of Sammy—as my daughter had asthma. They lived an hour away and didn't come often. I always vacuumed everything up and made sure Sam was put in the cat holder when they did visit, but I looked around for a good home for him. One of the ladies I worked with knew some people who would take him. So one day, my younger daughter, Stephanie, and I took Sammy to my coworker's home and left him there so he could be picked up by his new family. It broke my heart to say good-bye to him, but I thought he would love farm life. He would be wild and free and go out on adventures.

A few weeks later while I was in the kitchen, I felt an old familiar rub across my legs. I said, "Sammy?" That's when I knew he had passed. I cried.

A month later my niece came to visit, and she suggested we call the person we had given Sammy to. I said, "He's passed."

She said, "You don't know; let's find out."

We got hold of the lady who had taken him. She said that Sammy did not bond with them. He stuck up his nose to them and after a couple weeks left and didn't come back.

My dreams of Sammy having a happily ever after did not come to be. I had been happy thinking he was doing well and that he had died in a good place. I ended up feeling a great loss from his passing and believing he was trying to come home to me. I did find cat prints in my yard and porch, but thought nothing of it—maybe they were his. I will never know and, you know, after all that, my daughter never brought my grandson to see me. When they called to tell me they wouldn't be able to take him far for his first year, I was so upset. I had given up my soul pet, Sammy, when I could have kept him for another year.

He was my earthbound warrior who beckoned me to come and get him from his birth home in Debolt, and he stayed with me for as long as I needed him. I still have tears, even now, as I write these words.

—**Julia Oh** *is from Grande Prairie, AB. Julia is a grandmother of ten and a mother of four. She is a semiretired school teacher and artist, as well as a Reiki Master who aspires to publish a children's book one day.*

ANIMALS AS MESSENGERS

Affirmation: When I pay attention to the messages I am so lovingly given, I honor the messenger and I honor myself.

Disconnection

Weaving a web tighter and tighter,
Leaving only a semblance of light,
The fear keeps me stagnated,
Allowing only a brief glimpse into what might have been
Had my creation liberated me from suffering.

Anything out of sequence becomes a nemesis with which to contend.
I need order—without which I aspire to create disorder.
I renounce the chaos that follows as I detour from my destiny,
Witnessing my reality become destructive
As punishment becomes my reward.

Being devoid of attachment to that which offends me
And born of ageless wisdom, which purifies me,
I weave this endless profusion tighter and tighter
Until collapsing; I have nowhere to go but into the void,
Which is the beginning of my enlightenment!

BECOMING AWARE OF MESSAGES

One of the common ways in which animals show up is as a messenger. Messengers can forward communications from beyond, from deceased loved ones, as well as bring important information to you about something that is happening now. Animals may show up in dreams, in meditations, or during an energy session, or physically place themselves where you are sure to notice them.

It is often difficult to ignore animal messengers as they tend to appear in ways that are very noticeable. Of course, you may not see them as a courier, but assume something else is going on with them because they are acting in a way that is not typical behavior for their species. Although any animal can be a messenger, birds stand out in this area because of their proximity to the sky. They are thought to deliver messages from heaven. Once you realize the importance of animal messages, you become more aware of the messenger and are not able to easily dismiss rare sightings or unusual actions. I pay attention when a bird swoops down in front of my car while I am driving, or if I see a bear sitting on the road waiting until I come quite close before it runs off. I rarely spot a fox, but one day while driving, I saw three of them at different times.

One early morning quite a few years ago, I came out of my house, walked over to my car to start it, and was startled by a moose who was standing right beside the car. Once I spotted him, he casually walked off as if we greeted each other every morning. I felt as unafraid as he seemed to be.

One beautiful summer afternoon as I walked out to the pasture to visit with my horses, I was surprised to see two or three coyotes resting comfortably beside my ponies. When the coyotes spotted me, they quickly got up and ran across the field. My horses just remained lying down in the grass as if this was a common everyday occurrence—as it may well have been! It is these kinds of interactions that I recognize as being messages for me to pay attention to.

I have had many other encounters with animals in various ways, and a few stand out in my mind. Three of these incidents involve different birds: a raven, a hawk, and a blue jay. I will talk about the hawk and blue jaw encounters in this chapter.

As raven is my totem animal, that story will be included in the Totem chapter.

BIRDS

Although each type of bird has its own unique characteristics, they are collectively known as messengers. As messengers, they bring unconscious thoughts into our consciousness, allowing us to soar to new heights of vibration while increasing our knowledge of ourselves as spiritual beings. Birds can be persistent with their messages and often hang around until we *get* it.

Many species of birds are considered brassy and bold, but that is because they will take liberties in bringing our own wisdom to us, in spite of our feelings about them.

Birds are the bringers of new concepts and change. They help you to manifest new ideas and create the freedom to act on your intentions. When birds are hanging around you in a way that is unusual, expect your intuition to increase and new, positive energy to uplift you.

The following questions may help you gain some clarity when birds are showing up in your life:

Have you been moody and restless lately?

Have you been placing limits on yourself in any way?

Do you feel stuck emotionally or spiritually?

Are changes happening around you, but you feel unable to handle them?

Are you creating excuses around moving forward?

Do you have a fear of being too powerful or not powerful enough?

Have you found yourself feeling more attuned to other people's energies?

Are you having a difficult time starting or finishing a project?

·!!· ₃!!·

It was a warm morning in early July that was threatening to turn very hot by midday, as summer days tend to do in the Peace Country in Alberta, Canada. Our summers are usually quite short, so hot summer days are very welcome in this part of the country.

I decided to go outside and pick the mature strawberries, which were at risk of over-ripeness by the end of the day if the hot sun, shining like a garden spotlight, had its way. As I was bending over, concentrating on finding the ripe, red, juicy berries, I felt a bit of a weight on my back. It surprised but didn't scare me. At first, I thought it may have been one of the dogs trying to get my attention by putting their paws on me. I reached back and felt a slight movement as the weight was released. The flutter of wings grabbed my attention, and as I straightened fully up, I turned and looked behind me just in time to see a blue jay fly up onto a branch of a nearby tree.

As I stood there looking up at him, he stared back at me as if to say, "Tag, your turn." I began speaking to him, saying, "Thank you—I received your message." Throughout this short exchange, the blue jay's eyes didn't leave my face, but he immediately flew away once I had thanked him. So, what did he have to tell me? Well, I had been dabbling in a few projects at that time with no clear direction. He was telling me that it was time to release fears, get on with it, and finish what I had started.

The following story happened a few years later as a hawk showed up with a message for me.

I was busy around the house one day when I heard a loud thump coming from the front of the house. I hurried outside to see what had created the noise. I couldn't see anything at first but then noticed a hawk lying on the deck about three feet from me. He was not moving, so I slowly came closer to him until I was standing just inches away from where he was quietly resting.

He began to stir and sat up. I moved back a bit to give him some space and then watched him slowly begin to spread his wings and fly up to the deck railing. He sat on the railing for quite a while as I stood by the door and watched him. It was a fairly cool day. I was starting to feel the cold and wanted to go inside and grab a jacket but thought I had better hold my place and make sure he was okay. He kept sitting there looking at me. Finally, I realized that this was no ordinary hawk sighting.

Our deck is covered with an overhang, so he would have been able to see the boundaries, as the space between the railing and the overhang is not that large. Also, I realized that I had never seen a hawk around here before, so sightings, especially close encounters, were very rare.

He seemed to be doing all right now, as it had been about twenty minutes since I had first heard the noise of him hitting the wall, but still he sat. It wasn't until I said, "You must have a message for me, Mr. Hawk," that he flew away.

This messenger's whisper to me was one of awakening. The hawk showed me, through his actions, that I had flown through the barrier between sleeping (unconsciousness) and was awakening into consciousness. Although I may find the process slow, it is listening to my inner voice that will help me gain the momentum to fly.

The messages that are brought to us by animals are intimate and timely. They can be a symbol of hope and unconditional love from those who are no longer with us on the physical plane. These messages can help to raise the spirits of the bereaved, as they recognize that their loved ones have not left them completely but are still able to communicate in ways that leave no doubt in the receiver's mind that, although, the physical body may be gone, the spirit lives on.

The next two stories reflect communications from above and beyond. They were told to me by two different people in two separate incidents, although the stories have some similarity.

This first narrative is a family story.

Love Messages

My sister, Faith, who lost her eldest son, Alex, at a young age to muscular dystrophy, saw an eagle sitting on the railing of their deck shortly after his passing and felt it was a message to her from him. Both her and her husband took this sighting as a sign of Alex having the mobility to fly free of the restrictions of his physical body. In her son's memory, Faith had an eagle tattooed on her shoulder as a reminder of his new freedom to fly.

The following story was told to me by one of my Reiki students and, although not identical to the preceding one, it is eerily similar.

An eagle came the day my dad died and for three mornings sat in the tree in mom's yard. It was beautiful! I felt like my dad was there, and in the afternoons when the eagle flew, I knew my dad was flying free—free of cancer and all his pain.

After my dad's memorial service the eagle disappeared. Mom said that when she is low, sad, or not sure of something, an eagle appears. I think it gives her strength. At times I've seen an eagle, too, usually when I am struggling with something.

The next two stories also illustrate messages brought to the authors by birds.

The owl is considered to be one of the wisest of all birds and their presence often indicates prophetic wisdom. The messages they give are sometimes unnerving for the recipient, but as birds are indicative of altering our spiritual consciousness, they can help us to accept life as a continuous cycle of rebirth.

TIMELY WISDOM

Living in the snowy northern Peace Country, a person gets used to driving in the winter.

You expect to see many animals, including moose and deer, often attempting to cross the road as you are driving. As long as you have common sense, winter tires, a trusty vehicle, and emergency gear, you are good to go.

On a typical winter day, for our area, I drove to a neighboring city for a meeting. In the early evening dusk, I was heading home and thinking about an upcoming bridge I had to cross, one that was known for its steepness and slippery sections.

The roads had been dry and clear, so I was going the speed limit, around 100 km an hour. I was about halfway up an incline that led to the crest of a hill. Beyond this was the long downward curving approach to the bridge. I happened to glance in the driver's side mirror and saw an owl fly across the road behind my vehicle. It was a large bird, and I could see it clearly despite the low light. Without thinking about it, my foot eased up on the gas pedal, slowing the vehicle.

I thought about the meanings attributed to owls: wise, knowledgeable, and, in some cultures, foretelling of death. I wasn't scared, though—in fact I remember feeling excited and blessed that I had seen the owl.

At this point in my thoughts, I had reached the crest of the hill and could see beyond. There was a large semi-truck in the oncoming lane and there, in my lane, was an enormous bull moose! Braking hard, I was able to avoid hitting it. If it had not been for my owl friend slowing me down, I know I would have been going too fast to stop and may not have been around to tell this story.

—**Cheryl Frank**

MESSAGE RECEIVED

In the summer, my husband and I travel up north to the Yukon to work. I work part-time in town and then join my husband to work with him in the bush for a few days a week. One day we were on our way out to the bush, traveling on a dirt road that is little more than a trail, which follows a river as it winds through the mountains. As we were just about to round a corner, three owlets flew up alongside the trail beside us. They were beautiful, healthy-looking birds and looked full grown. I was thinking that they were just about to leave the nest to face the world on their own. We were amazed to see three at one time!

After four days of working in the bush, we headed back to town along the same winding trail. Rounding the same corner where we had initially seen the owls—imagine our surprise—when we saw all three of them again! This time, we stopped to admire them and take pictures for about fifteen minutes before they flew away.

After this second sighting, I felt that there was a message for us because it did not seem normal for owls to stay in the same place for any length of time once they had been spotted. We discussed the incredible experience of seeing the owls twice, and I was thinking to myself that owls are known to bring messages of death.

Then, another strange thing occurred. A beaver was sitting in the middle of the road, just watching our approach. He did not attempt to get off the road until we slowed down to keep from hitting him, and then he slowly wandered off as we passed him. Although it is common to see a beaver in the water, we have never seen one sit in the middle of the road like that. I took it as another sign to be interpreted.

As we live in a different part of the country in the winter, we try to see the friends who live here in the Yukon when we come out of the bush. I had been feeling guilty, as I had not yet visited them this summer, so I made a point of going to see them this time. As I walked into the house, I saw a good group of people already there. My friend immediately came up to me and whispered in my ear that their daughter-in-law had just passed away that day from a self-inflicted injury. It was devastating news, and I immediately thought of the owls and knew they had appeared to forewarn us. I also knew there would be more deaths to come.

That evening, we found out that another good friend of ours had been diagnosed with cancer and had a life expectancy of one year. He passed away less than a month later.

A few weeks later, we received news that a former classmate of my husband's had suddenly passed away from a heart attack.

In the meantime, I also realized the beaver's message. It was telling us that we are very much a part of this community, even though it is only for the summer months, and that it is important for us to help out as we would in any community we belong to. We became very involved in the local memorials as well as other community events that summer.

It has been five months since we saw the owls, and there have not been any more deaths. I sincerely believe the owls have delivered their message.

—**Loretta Zaluski** *resides near Hythe, Alberta, during the winter and in Mayo, Yukon, during the summer.*

This next story is one that brought immense comfort to the author by a message brought to her in an unusual way.

COMFORT IN A TIME OF NEED

On the day I returned from a three-week vacation in eastern Canada, I was stopped in my tracks as I was confronted by my two young adult children. They were crying as they waited for me on the front porch of my home. With sadness and tears in their eyes, they explained that our two-year-old blue heeler/beagle cross dog named Lexi, who I loved so deeply and was thinking about excitedly while driving home from the airport, was missing! According to all reports, she simply vanished. It was difficult to accept that nobody knew when or exactly how it had happened. At the time, I was rather optimistic that she would be found since she was not normally the kind of dog to ever take off. Even off-leash, she stayed close by.

The days passed without any sign of Lexi. It was as though she had disappeared without a trace. No one in the neighborhood had seen her.

Notices went out. All the usual places such as veterinarians, SPCAs, etc. had been contacted. I was beginning to feel panicky, as she had a blood condition and needed medication to survive.

I decided to call a dear friend of mine for help—a friend whom I admire and who I know is universally connected. She told me that she sensed Lexi was taking care of her own life and that I should thank and bless her for doing so. I wanted her to be wrong, but after considerable thought, I knew in my heart that she was right. I am so grateful for her wisdom. It really helped me to get through the darkest hours.

Several weeks later, when I had come to terms with the fact that Lexi was not coming home, I attended an outdoor yoga session in a beautiful wooded area close to town. Upon my arrival, I noticed a handsome dog belonging to the owner of the home. There was something about this dog that caught my attention, but I couldn't really place what it was. Not particularly friendly—the dog didn't appear to interact with any of the guests—but it seemed well-behaved. I got out of my car and carried on with my plans, which included a group yoga session followed by a labyrinth walk. Afterward, the approximately twenty yoga participants met in a circle back by the fire pit to visit and share stories.

Shortly after I sat down by the fire, I noticed the dog running from the house toward us. He trotted right across the circle of participants to sit directly in front of me. He was staring at me, and I reached out to gently pet him. I could see the owner was looking a bit shocked, and I later learned that this was certainly unusual behavior for her dog. But I knew right away that this dog came with a message. His purpose was clear. He provided me with comfort in my time of need. It was a message from my Lexi that she was okay.

When the owner stood up and said, "That's amazing!" I tried to explain—without becoming unglued—that I had just lost my dog, and her dog was acknowledging my sorrow and providing reassurance.

It seems that when something profound happens, our senses are alerted. We stop thinking and simply listen better. This was no coincidence!

I thank Lexi for her enduring love and my friend Tanis and the universe for helping me through this difficult time.

—**Dale Kardas,** *Grande Prairie, Alberta*

When messages come to us, it is for a reason. Sometimes we become so caught up in life that we virtually ignore what is happening right in front of us. If the message is important enough, the carrier will be persistent in getting it across. This next author tells us her story and what happened when she ignored the constant chattering going on all around her.

BE PREPARED IS NOT JUST A MOTTO FOR BOY SCOUTS

I live in the country and see animals all the time, so when I see an animal, I ask myself how I feel. If I feel calm and happy, I know that animal is there as nature intended. If I feel agitated, I know that the universe has sent that animal with a message, and my subconscious is trying to tell me something.

Such was the case when I was feeling really angry at all the squirrels that seemed to be plaguing me. Normally, squirrels are cute little things that frolic in the yard. However, lately, they seemed to irritate me, as I had squirrels in the bird feeders, squirrels chasing each other over the deck while I was trying to enjoy the sunshine, and they even started to throw acorns at me whenever I was in reach. I soon started to realize that they may be trying to tell me something, and when they were so bold as to get into my house, I knew that I should listen up! My book of animal spirit guides told me that I needed to get my house in order.[6] When I read that, I knew exactly what they had been trying to tell me. I was behind on doing my accounting and sending in the quarterly reports to the tax office, but I was so enjoying the summer that I procrastinated. I should have listened to them!

As my husband and I were finishing up our summer work season and packing up to head home, I got a call that my dad was in ICU, in the hospital, with pneumonia and other complications (he had picked up a super bug while in the hospital, and it destroyed his large intestine). We rushed down to be with him. We conducted all-day vigils with dad in ICU every day for over a week. I firmly believe that comatose patients can hear what is going on around them, as we could see the spike in Dad's vital signs when we arrived or when we talked directly to him.

When we were not at the hospital, we were spending time with my mom and supporting her through Dad's illness. Dad started to improve; he came out of the coma and was taken out of ICU a week later, although he was very weak and needed physiotherapy.

During this time, my husband started to have leg pains and within a week could no longer walk. We were fortunate enough to see the vascular surgeon in emergency, and the surgeon diagnosed my husband with having total blockage in his lower vascular arteries. He needed to have double bypass surgery and was told he had the arteries of an eighty-year-old man, even though he was only fifty-three. The universe has such immaculate timing, as we had just returned from our summer jobs working in the bush where there is no medical assistance for hundreds of miles. If this had happened when we were still in the bush, we would have been in very big trouble.

---

[6] Narayan Singh-Animal Activities: Their Psycho-Symbolic Meanings—A Shaman's Handbook

During the next week, my husband was having all the tests he needed completed in order to have his surgery, which was scheduled in ten days. Fortunately, both my dad and husband were in the same hospital, but on different floors. My days were filled with either helping dad with physiotherapy or spending time with my husband while he went through all the required tests. As you can see, I did not have any time to get my accounting done. The day of the surgery seemed to arrive very fast, and my husband came through the ordeal as well as could be expected.

While my husband was recuperating, we found out that my dad had gotten pneumonia again. The massive drugs they used to beat the superbug did not work anymore. My dad was not able to pull through this time.

The next few weeks were filled with looking after funeral arrangements and sorting financial issues. My mom was totally devastated. My parents had been together for fifty-six years, and mom was lost; it was very important to be there for her and help her find a life she could accept without dad.

I never told anyone, but during this time, I received the dreaded overdue notice stating that I had not filed my required quarterly return. I also received an additional notice as the next quarterly return was also overdue. Anyone who has dealt with Revenue Canada knows that their penalties are very expensive. With a very heavy heart, I called Revenue Canada and explained that I would not be able to complete the quarterly return for a while. They asked for a reason, and when I choked it out as best I could, they—to my amazement—were very understanding.

It took another month before my husband and I were able to leave my mom and get back to our own home where I could finally complete both quarterly returns.

The point of this long story is that the universe knows exactly what is coming. It uses animal guides to send us messages, and if we take the time to listen, believe, and follow through with whatever the message is, we will be better prepared and able to cope.

P.S. I never did receive a penalty from Revenue Canada, but I sure learned to listen to my animal spirits!

—Loretta Zaluski

Messages come in many forms from different situations. The animals in our lives never hesitate to deliver the information we need to know. We just have to become more aware of the messenger. Often, we already know our best course of action but just need that extra little push in order to make the changes that are necessary, to keep forging ahead on our path, as illustrated by Tania's story coming up next.

CLARITY STRAIGHT FROM THE HORSE'S MOUTH

I was in a pretty rough spot in my marriage, and I knew something had to change; I just didn't know how to make it happen.

One night as my husband and I were settling into bed, he wanted to talk. He told me how he had started to seek support from his sister and her husband since he and I weren't communicating anymore, like we should have been. He also told me what his family thought of our situation and explained that his sister and her husband thought he should just let me go, as they felt I was not worth the hassle. I heard what he said—loud and clear! After sitting for a moment and taking in what he had just told me, the tears started to fall. I was hurt—but not for me. I knew I was the one who was about to make a decision that would change our lives—I just didn't know how. He tried to console me because he thought his words had wounded me, and then he comforted me by saying he didn't agree with what his family had said. I stopped him from saying anything else and made it very clear that the tears were not for me because of what he had said; the tears were for him. My heart broke as I realized that those people were his support system if he didn't have me in his life. My situation became very real in that moment.

Although my husband didn't want me to, I had to leave to clear my head. I'm certain he didn't understand why I needed to regain my thoughts. I got into my new vehicle and started to drive. As I headed out east of town, I started crying again. In my heart I knew my marriage was over, and at that moment, I resented him more than I knew how to deal with. He wasn't a husband to me anymore, and I felt very alone.

As I was driving, I turned down a gravel road heading north and—out of nowhere—I saw two glowing eyes coming straight for me, without hesitation and with no intention of stopping. My initial thought was about my new vehicle ... so I stopped ... and I waited. The eyes kept coming toward me, then hesitated, as if to say, *look at me* and *pay attention*! As I sat there, watching with amazement, I saw a big, beautiful, chestnut horse turn into a cutline. In that moment, I realized I had been given a sign, and immediately I stopped crying. I had grown up with horses my entire life; they represent freedom to me, and they allow a person to be who they truly are.

After that, I knew what I needed to do; it was like clarity had come over me that no matter the cost, I had to be true to myself.

When I returned home, my husband was worried sick, as I had been gone for quite some time. He asked what had happened and where I had gone, so I told him about encountering the horse and how I was feeling. I don't think he believed me, but then ... in my next breath, I told him I was done and that I couldn't live this way anymore.

—**Tania Hicks**

ANIMALS AS TEACHERS

Affirmation: When I recognize my teachers, their wisdom and divine knowledge give me the answers my body, mind, and soul have asked for, allowing me to become more powerful in my manifestations.

Without Limits

The rebellious power exhilarates me.
I recognize the strength with which we stride
Effortlessly across the visible plain.

Beneath me, the animal surges ahead, a free spirit without restraint,
Its limitless action reminding me of my divinity,
Enhanced by each pound of the hoof as it
reflects the rhythm of my heartbeat.

The dissolution of my humanity becomes
the choice I make as I lose myself,
Realizing the context of this moment has no time or place—
Only the space to recognize my spirit.

As one, we are noble in our pursuit of the unknown,
Caring not what transpires beyond this time, only acknowledging
Resources that lead us to the humble manifestation of our destiny.

Slowing, we bring the unconscious back into consciousness again,
After sharing the wisdom of the ages in a connected vision,
And breathe in the knowledge that transformed two into one.

LESSON PLAN

Animals come into our lives to teach us something about ourselves. As any pet owner knows, the lessons can be ongoing—especially if we aren't paying attention.

The type of animal you choose to *own* is reflective of yourself and the lessons you need to learn. As illustrated by some earlier stories in this book, the animal often chooses you, rather than you choosing it.

Dogs teach us about loyalty and playfulness. Cats show us how to be independent and ask for what we want. Birds signify wanting to access information beyond the physical, and horses indicate a need for power and freedom. These tend to be the most relatable animal species, but fish, insects, and reptiles also have a lesson to impart.

Fish teach us about perseverance; insects show us communication and co-operation strategies; and reptiles give us knowledge about releasing the old and embracing the new.

Each creature that comes into your life helps you to realize something about yourself if you take the time to *hear* what it has to say. Often the teachers move on as the lesson is completed with them, but sometimes the connection is so strong that their energy lingers or comes back in another form.

There are short-term connections as well as long-term commitments, as in the case of many wild animal encounters. The short-term lessons are more immediate and may relate to *at this particular time in your life*, rather than an ongoing teaching.

Whatever the case may be, it is important to be aware of those moments that the animal honors you with its presence. All it asks of you in return is unconditional love and acceptance. A simple *thank-you* is a tribute that shows respect for the time any animal has spent with you.

HORSES

Having had horses most of my life, I have become accustomed to the various personalities they possess. Each horse is unique in character, which makes them brilliant teachers, as they individually respond to people differently. As well, they are very intuitive and can read people easily. They react to emotions, and if you become very connected to a specific horse, it will almost be able to read your mind. That, to me, is the most freeing experience I have ever had—the ability to be so attuned to your horse, and it to you, that no words or actions are necessary.

The horse has been characterized as a romantic animal since historical times, and its versatility is legendary. It has been a companion, a mode of transportation, and a partner in conflicts. There has had to be absolute trust between the horse and rider in order to accomplish many historical feats, as the horse was wholly depended upon during life defying activities.

Once free to roam the range (still do in some areas), horses represent being free, rebellious spirits. Man has attempted to tame this beast and has in a lot of instances, but not without effort. I can remember my dad regaling me with stories of *breaking* horses. *Breaking* is an apt term, as humans literally used to break the will or spirit of the horse by catching, teaching it to lead, saddling, and riding this beautiful animal, often all in one day. Today we tend to use more gentle means of bending it to our will.

I believe horses are very willing animals as long as we respect what they stand for.

Horses in your life may be asking you:

Are you being playful enough?

Are you accepting of your own power?

Is your rebelliousness taking you where you want to go?

Are you respecting of the earth and giving gratitude for what it provides you?

Do you have wisdom to share but hesitate to do so because of fear of rejection?

Are your manifestations reflective of who you are, or are they a reflection of collective consciousness beliefs?

Are you afraid of success because it will bring more responsibility into your life than you think you can handle?

One of the most precocious horses I have ever owned was Cocheise. I bought him from an uncle of mine when he was about twelve years old. He was the most stubborn horse I have ever known, but he was also one of the wisest teachers I ever had. I think he taught me patience above all else. He loved to play games and, although I became very exasperated at some of his antics, he taught me how to laugh at myself.

Cocheise always seemed to know when I was coming out to catch him to go riding or if he was just going to get some attention with a brushing and a treat. The treat and brushing Cocheise willingly came for. When it was time for a ride, well, that was an entirely different story. It didn't matter if I displayed the halter or hid it, he always knew. I thought I had him fooled by carrying a piece of twine in my pocket in order to catch him, but that didn't work after the first time I tried it. I would pretend to be nonchalant and not care if I caught him or not—he just seemed to laugh at that ploy. I followed the suggestion of my farrier[7] who said, "Just carry the halter up to him and if he runs away, throw

---

[7] A person who takes care of the hooves of animals.

it at him and keep him running; he will eventually tire and stop." Oh, sure, if it came to a running contest between me and a horse, who do you think will win? Truth is, I did keep at it until I eventually caught him—never did let him get away with it—but after chasing a horse for a good hour, who has the energy to go riding?

The funny thing is that he liked to get out of the corral and ride out in the bush on the trails. Once he was caught, he was almost a perfect ride … almost, but it all depended on who was riding him and how far we were going! He seemed to love green riders[8]—not that he ever consciously hurt them, but he could tease. He would just halt in mid-stride and no amount of coaxing would get him going again unless he was headed in the direction of home—then not much could stop him.

Cocheise loved to get into the bush and slowly turn us around until we were headed toward home. The trouble was that he would immediately begin to walk or trot faster as soon as he was pointed in the direction he wanted to go, alerting us to the fact that we were going home. If we ever got lost, though, it was Cocheise who found the way back.

I never knew another horse that could walk so painfully slow going one way, so much so that everyone had to wait for him, or walk so quickly going home that all the other horses had to trot or lope to keep up to him.

Even with all the seeming trouble Cocheise appeared to be, he was the one horse I could trust with new or inexperienced riders. I knew he would teach them how to ride, how to have patience, and more about themselves than they may have wanted to know.

Several incidents with this often frustrating creature led me to realize what an exceptional gentle teacher Cocheise was. The following is one event I remember vividly.

---

[8]   Individuals who have very little experience riding a horse.

On a camping trip with friends several years ago in the beautiful Kakwa region in Alberta, three of us were riding along the trails when we came to a clearing. Cocheise and I were in the lead, and I spotted a brown shape at the other end of the meadow. Riding a bit closer, we recognized that we were in the company of a large grizzly bear, which are abundant in that area. Reacting in fear, we all turned our horses and headed back to camp at a run. After a few moments, I felt Cocheise stumble and then fall. It happened so fast that I was unable to respond quickly enough to take any action. As he fell, I felt pressure on my left side when he landed. I remember thinking he was going to fall right on me. That light pressure I felt when Cocheise first fell was all I noticed, as he promptly lifted himself off of me by rolling so he was sitting upright. As it turned out, he had lost a horseshoe, which created the imbalance and, subsequently, the fall occurred.

His concern for me was very heartwarming, and although I had known it before this incident happened, this was further proof of his gentle character.

When Cocheise passed in 2011, it was a sad day for many. That gentle teacher who had so much to give was gone. I have had many horses in my life, and I have loved them all, but Cocheise was a character who will not soon be forgotten.

When I would tell my uncle (Cocheise's former owner) stories about this often exasperating character, he would laugh and say, "You just have to be smarter than the horse!" That would definitely work in many instances, but it was difficult to outsmart the infamous Cocheise, which made him one fabulous teacher.

We can find teachers anywhere we choose to look in nature.

Join Carrie in this next story as she tells you about taking an hour out of her day to learn powerful lessons from a *teenage* bumblebee.

Bumblebee ER

My mom was visiting from Cape Breton, and we were out cleaning the deck with soapy water to get the winter grime off. We had a bowl of warm, soapy water on the table, and then Ma says, "Oh look! A mosquito fell in the bubbles and is stuck."

Well, I figure there is no way a mosquito is that big for her to see in the bubbles, so *Miss Vegan* here rushes over to investigate. My mother is not as detail oriented as I am, as far as animal/insect identification … so low and behold, it looks to me like a young bumblebee. Well, I snap into 911 paramedic mode! Oh my, a precious bumblebee is stuck in soapy water. This isn't good.

I grab a pair of scissors and put them under him so he can find some solid ground among the *bubble clouds* he was trying to stand on. He finally does … so he's safely out of this bubble mess. I yell to Ma to go get my spray bottle under the bathroom sink so I can mist off the bubble residue to give him a fighting chance. Bumblebees are so important, I know, so this case is a true emergency. She yells to me that the spray bottle says plant food, and I am certain it is not, so I say, "Yeah, that's good."

I put Mr. Bumblebee, who is clinging to the handle of my scissors, into the planter box. It was topped with mulch, so I could easily monitor him and make sure he was okay while I misted.

Ma had asked, "Should I empty the bottle and fill it with warm water?" I figured that the water in it would be room temperature and that would be better for him.

I frantically start to spray off the bubble residue as I am watching him struggle—walking around and moving like he was confused. He did just fly into a *ginormous* vat of dish soap, so he's got to be dazed, stunned, and frantic, of course. Anyone who has had sticky soap on them before—especially in their eyes—can appreciate what he must have been going through … the poor thing.

Well, to my surprise, as I am spraying like mad to make a little shower for him to wash the dish soap off, I scream "Oh my God!" as I remember that although this says plant food from another time, and I knew it wasn't that … I did forget that I decided to use the spray bottle for a vinegar orange mix I made up to clean out the tub and sink (rather than use cleaning chemicals). When Ma had asked me if this was just water when she first grabbed it, I had forgotten that part.

Oh no! In attempting to save this beautiful creature, who fell in a bowl of dish soap originally, I unknowingly gave him a lovely misted shower of *vinegar and orange* mixture. Yes, two very sticky and yucky substances like that, unlike the *water I meant to use* to wash away the dish soap, was not the best course of treatment by any means. By this time I am frenzied at what I just did, in trying to *save Mr. Bumblebee*. Well, to say I was freaking was an understatement. To some they would say, "Well, let nature take its course, and if he lives, he lives." Well, "Grey's Anatomy" has nothing on me in the ER.

I yelled to Ma when I realized what I had just *soaked* him in.

She replied, "Yes, I can smell it." So while she ran to rinse out the bottle and put *actual water* in it this time, I was making sure he didn't crawl out of the planter box. He was just wandering around and around. I couldn't believe that in trying to save the little guy from a dish soap bath, I added a nice bath of vinegar and oranges to the mix.

By this time, I thought his chances of survival were slim to none, really. What a mess I had created!

Finally, with *actual water* in hand, I quickly misted again with the warm water in hopes that it would all wash off eventually. Bees don't really like being misted (FYI), so he kept wandering around as if to get away from the water. He probably was thinking, *What next—an oil bath? Because if I had of known about how this day would turn out, I would have rolled over, hit the snooze button, and stayed in the hive.*

I was thinking that if the materials he had on his body don't kill him, I'm sure he'll die of a heart attack from all the stress I was putting him through. And for a moment, I thought, although I like Angelina Jolie's big voluptuous lips, I do not want to be stung while attempting to give mouth-to-mouth resuscitation if his little bee's heart stops. I was actually laughing out loud while I was thinking of the cartoon of it all happening.

So after the thorough misting shower of clean water, I just watched and waited to see what he would do next. I figured he needed a break from it all. I put the scissor handles near him, and he crawled back on them again, almost as if it was a life preserver that he recognized. By this point, he seemed to slow down. I could see him start to rub his little front legs up his antenna as if to dry them off. He was also attempting to clean his eyes off. I figured it must be hard to hold onto the scissors and dry yourself off at the same time (now that's multi-tasking at its best), so I grabbed a flat rock I had on the deck for him to rest on. Now he was safely in the sun, on solid ground, and he could do what needed to be done.

Well, I decided to simply sit and watch him do his necessary preening routine. He was smaller with less hair than the regular sized bumblebees I am used to seeing. I don't know much about the stages of bumblebees, but I made the assumption that he was a juvenile. You could actually see the little yellow and black hairs on his body, legs, and head. Well, he spent the next twenty minutes just drying himself off and getting himself moving. It was amazing to watch his various legs completely go over his entire body. He moved his abdomen and thorax like crazy. He was even balancing on his head, using his front legs stretched to the side, while he rolled his *large* abdomen around—almost defying gravity.

It was so Zen-like that I felt like I was intruding on his own personal yoga routine.

Every now and again, he would try to flap one wing, and I would shout to Ma, almost as if I was a proud mama watching her baby take his first steps. I felt as long as he could get his wings going, he would be home free—back to the hive. What a story he would have to tell the queen!

It appeared that one wing was not flapping like the other one, so I figured I would do the water mist thing again for a bit, in case there was some sticky residue still on his other wing. They looked so delicate, and I got some great pictures of how see-through and thin they really are. He started walking around again on the rock as if he didn't like the mist, but then he just settled again and went back to cleaning himself off. After a while, he did start moving that other wing and flapping both of them in little attempts—just making sure they were working properly. We were so excited every time he did that, as it seemed more hopeful that he could actually make it through this rough ordeal he was experiencing.

I took various pictures and videos while I was enjoying this real life movie. It was an *in the moment* kind of time where I kept wondering if he could recover and what would become of him. I passed the camera back to my mother and continued to be fascinated, watching as he went on with his sunbathing routine. Life is amazing! In the blink of an eye (we were watching him one moment and the next, without any warning), he just took flight to the air, and we saw him quickly fly off. It was the coolest moment, and we yelled, "Did you see that?" to each other. There was no warning of him starting his engines; he just simply took off. I guess the long time he spent rubbing off the dish soap, vinegar, oranges, and finally that water really paid off. It was the most incredible thing to witness, and we were both in disbelief at how quickly he just up and left. It was a sight to see! With his obvious strength and determination, I would like to think that he made it back to his hive and spent that night reliving the whole experience with his worker buddies over a cup of honey.

Taking the time out of my day to simply sit and be in the moment was truly very therapeutic for me. Watching nature, one can't help but believe that there must be a God or Creator of the many beautiful and unique things that are blessed to live on this earth. It is truly magnificent to enter the world of creatures that surround us and take the time to stop and smell the roses, or in this case, stop and watch the teenage bee take a few baths.

I am proud that I am the kind of person who is helpful to others regardless of their size and species. If the tables were reversed, I would like to think that animals would do the same for us. Yes, it was only one little bee, but it was a bee that came to my deck and allowed me into his life for a brief moment in time. I know from learning about bees that they are master pollinators, assisting with the reproductive cycle of plants. And this goes beyond the beauty of flowers; their pollinating powers impact important crops of all kinds. Bees play a key role in the delicate balance of our ecosystem.[9] It was so important for me to help save one of these important bees if I could. Watching this little guy finally overcome the obstacles he faced gave me sort of a spiritual meaning to glean from this experience. The dish soap was an unfortunate circumstance. The vinegar orange spray, supposed to be water, was not meant to be anything other than helpful. It forced him to stop what he was doing in his day, to take time to get back on his feet, strengthen his wings, and take flight again, leaving his struggle behind. That is what I am taking from my brief hour with Mr. Teenage Bumblebee. He reminds me of my resilience in the face of struggles I have in my own life. Deal with what is, calmly make a plan, take the necessary time to regroup, and move forward in flight to your next adventure. I believe life gives us what we need when we need it. We can

---

[9]   http://www.psychicsuniverse.com/articles/spirituality/living-spiritual-life/
spiritual-power-humble-bee

learn lessons in many unique and unorthodox ways. We just have to be open to the possibilities and be willing to take the time to see them.

In looking up the meaning of bumblebees, I found this.[10] Bumblebees are miraculous. Theoretically they are unable to fly—but do. The bee is asking you to contribute to the collective raising of the vibration of the earth. Forget about impossibility, and allow miracles to manifest in your life.

—**Carrie Currie** *is a school teacher living in Halifax, Nova Scotia, and very proud to have her roots come from good old Cape Breton. Even as a child, she grew up always having a love and respect for nature with its many creatures, big and small. She has been a proud mama to many fish, a gerbil, a rabbit, three hamsters, three rats (yes, rats make the most amazing pets), and two dogs, and has rescued many injured animals and brought them to Hope for Wildlife for rehabilitation back to the wild. She loves to be in nature as much as she can: hiking, camping, making labyrinths at numerous beaches, or just simply communing with good ol' Mother Nature. Making the decision to go vegetarian, three years ago, was the best decision for her. It has been a huge learning curve in educating herself to further live a healthy lifestyle. She has been transitioning to the vegan lifestyle a year ago January past. Her decision to fully eat vegan makes her very proud. She truly believes the life of an insect is just as valuable as the life of any larger living being that lives upon this earth. She is now truly committed to avoid the use of all products tested on animals, as well as animal-derived nonfood products in her daily life. She is thankful for the many blessings in her life and gives back to people whenever she can. Her favorite pastimes include bargain and thrift store shopping for anything she can craft and recycle into something else. She is a true crafter and creative person by nature. She values art in its many forms and fills her home with items that represent the spirit of artists on this same journey.*

---

[10]   http://www.psychicsuniverse.com/articles/spirituality/living-spiritual-life/spiritual-power-humble-bee

The following story illustrates how our perception of a certain animal can change with our experience of it. Cats, as most animals do, respond to our energy. They act out our feelings at a subconscious level in order to bring to us the message we most need to hear. Even though the cats in this story are family pets, the two young men within the family are the designated owners of a cat each. The cats display the personalities of their individual teen owners with Oreo being quite shy and reclusive, disappearing when a stranger appears, much like her owner. Snuggles is much bolder and protective like her pet-parent. Even though these cats tend to exaggerate the qualities of their human family, they create a reflection of the individual characters.

My Feline Teachers

I was sitting in a public house in my university town of Leicestershire, United Kingdom, completely minding my own business, when this big, fat, orange cat—much resembling Garfield—jumped into my lap. Surprised and somewhat flattered by this unexpected and unusual show of affection, I proceeded to run my fingers along its long, sleek coat. No sooner had my fingers touched its coat when it turned around, bit me, and then leapt away.

As I began to slowly process what had just happened, anger raised its ugly head. I became convinced that cats couldn't be trusted. They were conniving, sly, unpredictable vermin, maybe good for the Egyptians but not for this Brit.

How is it then, over twenty years later, I find myself head over heels with not one but two of these cuddly calico creatures? What was it that I saw in my feline nemesis? And why is it I refer to them as my feline teachers?

I find that their presence fills me with joy and hope, often because I can't find it in myself and need the reminder that it exists.

I never thought I could love again—not until the grandchildren came, that is. I didn't think that I had more love to give. Since my boys were born, I thought they had the monopoly on that, but these creatures have taught me that my love is bountiful, endless, and timeless. I find myself bewitched, bewildered, and bedazzled by them.

With their strong, streamlined bodies, so soft and warm, lying stretched out at my feet, they smile at me knowingly, recognizing what I am only just discovering.

There's no unconditional love here, not on their terms anyway—not like their canine enemies. They never wait by the door when I get home after a twelve-hour shift, happy to see me—they're indifferent. They simply stare and continue on with their journey, aloof and unconcerned, yet powerful in their strength. But I know it's just that this love is more subtle; they don't need to display any grand shows of affection or gestures to demonstrate their gratitude. They show me that just by allowing me to be in their presence how blessed I am.

They have taught me the gift of independence and how to become my own best friend; they have taught me that without this ability, all other avenues are fruitless in their pursuit. They have taught me that the only real love that I should ever crave is that of my own, for myself—it is really all I ever need.

They have taught me the fruitlessness of self-pity and need by turning their noses and walking briskly off in the other direction when these traits should raise their ugly head. Yet, when I am strong and happy, they jump into my arms longing for my embrace as if rewarding me for displaying more favorable attributes.

They have taught me to pursue my dreams and continue on with my heart's desires—regardless of the consequences—because others soon forget and forgive your mistakes, but will you ever forgive yourself for having missed the opportunity to make them?

They force me to be present, to be fully aware and awakened in this remarkable moment, to share the perfection of life with every breath. They forgive me in an instant when I accidently step on their tail. Finding my remorse unnecessary, they have forgiven me long before I have forgiven myself.

How is it that they can say so much with saying so little? They teach me that words aren't always necessary, but silence is golden, supreme and powerful.

I do not expect others to understand this connection we have—this deep, spiritual connection—they see only the surface of the feline beauty. How can they know the lessons I have been taught and how deep our bond has grown? How can they know the adoration and love I see and feel in every look, in every moment, in every sweet subtle smile?

My fantastic, fabulous, furry, feline teachers have taught me much more than I thought I ever needed to learn: joy, acceptance, self-worth, forgiveness, independence, strength, and peace—far more than any human being has ever done!

—**Arinder Sanun** *is originally from the United Kingdom, but now lives in Grande Prairie, Alberta, with her husband, her two boys, and their two cats.*

A good teacher not only gives you new information to digest, but allows you to process it on your own terms. Depending on where you are in your life, you tend to only see what you need to, at the time you receive the information. Subconscious limiting beliefs only allow you to see as far as the results of your experiences.[11] Once you release those buried

---

[11] Deep Cellular Healing is a modality that helps you to identify any limiting subconscious beliefs and release them easily and permanently, moving you forward into new opportunities and experiences.

beliefs, you open up to a new perspective, gaining clarity and ensuring a new beginning, as Elisa explains in the following story.

LOOKING THROUGH THE NEW EYES OF NATURE

New beginnings come—often when something ends. New beginnings also come when we have new eyes in which to see the world.

As I begin to write these words, I can feel my heart beating in my chest. I feel excited, yet anxious, and full of emotion from the words that would like to escape from inside of me. I write often in daily emails, communicating for work, personal life, and volunteer positions. However, when I am inspired to write from my soul, it evokes a lot more feeling. It feels as though I am encountering a new adventure as I begin to believe in my own inner guidance, which at one point seemed untrustworthy. It has grown to where I believe that I can finally start to make a difference and hope that this, my first journey of words, will inspire another person to look at the world differently and grow.

I am not entirely sure when I first began to notice how animals and nature impacted my daily life. About thirteen to fifteen years ago, I recall reading a book called *Animal Speak* by Ted Andrews,[12] where he described many animals and the meaning of an encounter with a specific animal. It was really fascinating to see how one could interpret seeing a certain animal and how we could learn from this to help us in our day-to-day lives.

Our family lives in the country, so wildlife is a common sight. When I was a new mom, I was challenged with listening to my intuition and recall one particular day when I was afraid and upset about something and noticed that outside in the yard stood a cow moose and her new

---

[12]   Animal Speak: The Spiritual & Magical Powers of Creatures Great and Small, Llewellyn Worldwide; 1993

adorable calf. The sun was shining, the sky was blue, and it was a beautiful sight to behold—such a healthy pair of animals. I was then pushed to go and find that interesting *Animal Speak* book again to investigate the meaning of their presence and read about how the moose shows us how to open up to our feminine energy. Moose are a very strong animal and have the ability to survive through the toughest aspects that nature can throw out. What I took away from the words I read that day helped me to trust myself a little more. I returned to that same book a few more times over the next while and started to associate the sighting of the moose with the fact that I was going to be challenged by something, and that I was going to have to *go down into the depths of the swamp or near death* to learn something, before I would be able to *climb out again with new strength and nourishment*. Instead of a positive interpretation, unfortunately, I constructed a negative one, believing that more struggle and pain was forthcoming! Over the next ten years, I started to secretly fear a moose encounter because of the belief that I had associated it with. Whenever the moose showed up in my life, I could feel fear clutching in my chest and throat as the anxious anticipation that something bad was about to happen came over me. Even further to this belief was that the *bad stuff* usually wasn't able to resolve itself and turn around again until another moose sighting had occurred, showing me that I had survived the swamp and was safe again! Was I going crazy? I eventually learned that the fear of something happening, or fear itself, just invites more fear and things to fear. It is like a boomerang that comes right back to you!

In the past year, many verbal quotes, literature, and discussions seemed to have come my way with the message that our beliefs are, in fact, just that—a belief. Yet, the fears I held were just hard to let go of.

It wasn't, however, until the first weekend of November 2013 that everything was put to the test. I was listening to an audio selection in the truck as we were beginning a six-hour drive home from a sporting event in Edmonton, Alberta. It pointed out that when we are faced with circumstances that feel negative, we have the opportunity to use *gratitude* for the silver linings that are hiding within them. These circumstances are also given to us to allow us to experience, announce, and declare who we really are. Finally, I was beginning to understand that my belief of struggle continuously occurring was the negative way to look at it. As we were driving down the back roads through the country, my husband happily pointed out to our family that there, in the field off to my left, stood a cow moose and her calf. My first instinct was not to look. *Here we go again*, is what my old belief was thinking— *the bad omen is showing up again.*

Earlier that week, our old tomcat had passed away, and the children were quite upset about it, as was I. I really did love that cat and was just as sad as they were. It also seemed like the last couple of months since school had gone back in that there were a lot of new challenges that the family faced. I have to say that I was just tired and in need of a rest. So when this moose sighting showed up, I instantly thought, *What else—what else are you going to throw at me?* My heart felt tight, and I just secretly wanted to cry. With nowhere else to turn, the impulse came to me to use my phone to scan the Internet for the meaning of moose medicine. Much to my surprise, words appeared that have forever changed my belief. They must have been there all along, but I had never read them in such a way, probably because the belief that I had about challenging circumstances was a negative one. Reading the words that day, with the new eyes that I had been inspired to look from, as a result of the audio selection that I had just listened to, allowed me to understand what the moose has always been trying to tell me. This was my *aha!* moment. I could almost feel relief gushing out of my body and peace enveloping me. Tears secretly burned in my eyes.

What was really happening as I began to interpret life through positive eyes is that I was having an opportunity to grow and evolve with each circumstance that I encountered. It was time to start welcoming life and enjoying it instead of being afraid of what was around the next corner. Finally, I was seeing the moose as the opportunity for me to be a better me. Circumstances were just circumstances, and they give us the opportunity to grow and learn, if we look at them in a positive way.

The moose energy is one of strength, self-esteem, courage, expression of joy when something has been accomplished, primal feminine energy, and magic of life and death, to name a few. Their cycle of power is late fall and early winter.

I now see the moose as my good luck charm as it walks through the field. It reminds me to be joyful no matter what the situation is, and it is just giving me another moment and another chance to experience, announce, declare, and become a new and improved version of myself, which is stronger, happier, kinder, more patient, and confident. Believe me, I still have a lot of ways I want to improve on a daily basis, and reminders keep coming to help me keep on track! Our journey is one of learning without having to sacrifice the fun of it, and if we pay attention to nature with new eyes, which are the window to our soul, we can see our interactions as advice to help us along our way.

—**Elisa Marie** *lives in northern B.C. with her family.*

When Debbi saw a fawn outside her window one winter morning, it became a learning moment for her. Often, seemingly ordinary events can become more—depending on how open we are at that time. Life's teachable moments are born of our ability to recognize them.

Little Strides

It's Sunday morning and a deep carpet of snow covers the ground.

I gaze out of my living room window into pristine whiteness.

Peace. Stillness.

Until …

In the snow I see something brown and animated move.

A baby deer is trapped in the neighbor's back yard, and they are away! Immediately I think of their dog, Butch, and pray he is with them. He'll likely go crazy and attack the poor baby.

But, no—they've gone away. I reassure myself that Butch usually goes with them. So far, no barking. The fawn's safe.

Until …

I watch closely as the fawn makes a run at the fence. He seems wobbly on his new, long, spindly legs. As if puzzled by his predicament, he runs at the fence from another angle but is no luckier. He skids to a stop as the snow sprays around him. If I didn't know better, he could be a kid at play.

I continue to watch, spellbound, as the little creature makes more and more attempts to vault over the fence. Determined, he does not back down. Standing still, he assesses his chances. He makes yet another try.

With the cold, frosty air biting his nostrils, he paces. As he lifts one trembling leg off the snow covered ground, his whole body quivers.

He waits.

His black velvety nose nuzzles the ground.

He tries to squeeze a taste from a half frozen corn cob.

Then he waits. Wary.

I try to beam my thoughts to him.

Elevate, go higher, get to the top by any and all means.

Piles of cushions.

A big footstool.

Long ladder.

Ramp.

If only I had a forklift!

As I watch him struggle, I wonder where this little animal came from. How did he get here? Did anyone else see him on the way?

Maybe the mother deer had been searching for food and in an effort to protect her young had hidden them in the underbrush, and this little one went astray. Why didn't he stay closer to his mother when in the forest?

How many miles had he traveled? What perils had he faced on his way out of the woods? Instead of being in this unfamiliar part of town, he should be in the countryside frolicking in the snow with his friends.

But now his body language says it all. He hangs his head. Forlorn.

He hoofs the snow like he's desolate, alone, and lost.

Then, once again, like a runner with second wind, the baby deer attempts to jump.

I worry more.

He's exhausted. Perhaps he will break his leg next. Then what?

He is helpless.

I am helpless.

His tentative steps echo my thoughts: the fenced in yard had become a prison.

How to break out?

Then I think of Jack, our friendly town councilor.

He is the compassionate type.

Yes, make a call. Now!

"Jack, you won't believe this." As we talk, I keep my eyes on the unfolding scene. "There's a baby deer in my neighbor's backyard. He's stuck behind the fence, and they're away. Thank God their dog is with them."

"Okay," says Jack. "How long has he been there?"

The fawn's bewildered, wild looking. I watch as he walks the perimeter of the yard.

"I have no idea. He was already there when I looked outside."

"Okay, then, maybe I can get a rope and ladder and I'll take the truck. You know your neighbor, Al, used to work for The Department of Lands and Forests. Why don't I pick him up on the way?"

"Please hurry, I am afraid for him; he's very young and could hurt himself. But it's worth a try," I say.

As we are making half-baked plans for the rescue of this inmate, I look out the window again.

The fawn paces, runs, makes one last leap, and goes straight over the fence.

I'm so excited that I drop the phone.

With his newfound, boundless energy, the fawn sprints across the road and through the adjacent fields into a thicket of trees.

I press my face to the windowpane.

I whisper, "Today you have been my teacher."

What did I discover today? *The old adage is true: if at first you don't succeed, try, try again.* This day my little forest friend taught me that success depends upon many attempts (not just one).

—**Debbi J. Helm** *is a graduate of St. Francis Xavier University (B.A., 1975; B.Ed., 1976). She works in Celtic Collections, St. Francis Xavier University, Antigonish, Nova Scotia, Canada.*

Facing your fears is one of the decisions that can change your life as you know it … forever. Join Pearl as she tells you about the weekend she spent immersed in learning to conquer her fears and how the days she spent in the wild changed her life. You cannot help but be impacted by this story and the courage she displayed in taking this step—not to mention what she learned about herself.

WILD WOMAN WEEKEND

Two summers ago I attended an event titled *Wild Woman Weekend.* I knew from the brief description of it in the brochure that the weekend would be way outside my comfort zone. But, eventually, I decided that's what I wanted! The past two years of my life had been almost completely outside of my comfort zone, on purpose, because it was time for some big personal growth. I couldn't grow while staying within my comfort zone, and I found that I still had a lot of fear inside me. I had been thinking that I would like to be more involved with horses, as they are one of my fears, but I hadn't had a chance yet. Some of my other fears are: falling off anything (even a step stool), the dark, bears, and sharing my innermost feelings (with anyone really).

I went to Wild Woman Weekend with high hopes and huge trepidation of what I would find.

After an opening circle greeting, the first thing we did was choose a horse to ride! I discovered that the horse actually chose me, instead of me choosing him. We rode bareback, without reins, while being led (phew!) And *blindfolded!* It was a completely *freeing* experience for me—and also for my hips—which loosened up wonderfully.

Unfortunately, it was just a short ride. After we dismounted, we stayed blindfolded and learned to walk together silently into the wilderness, all holding the same rope. Then, still blindfolded, we crawled silently on a path, going deeper into the wild, individually going at our own speed. I felt like a bear lumbering along. I was having no trouble staying on the path and was very aware that there was someone close by to keep me from straying too far. We crawled for a long way, *long* past the point where I would have stopped due to discomfort.

Eventually we were each led, walking, to a sandbar beside a stream. There we were allowed to remove the blindfolds and share our experiences. I learned that each of us had experienced a different animal, and that our leader had been able to observe each of us shape-shift.[13] So amazing!

A short while later, we hiked along beside the stream that recently had become a river due to excessive rainfall in June and July. At different points on our hike, we splashed back and forth across the unnavigable spots. We had to search for hand and footholds while making our way across steep parts of the bank. (Me?)

---

[13]   Shape-shifting is allowing your energy to merge with that of an energy with similar traits, becoming as one.

After a while, we reached our cooking spot. We learned to start a fire using fuel available in the area and a flint. Success makes wild rice very tasty!

While supper was cooking, and for a long time later, we all shared parts of ourselves with the others. We did more shape-shifting and some drumming and dancing, while thanking the world around us for its bounty! We watched the moon rise and turn the riverbanks silver. Then we watched the sky darken with clouds as the lightning crept closer. As the rain began to fall, we started our trek back to the sleeping spot.

So in the dark, in the pouring rain, in the lightning and thunder, we completed our circle of travel along the stream, up a grassy cliff—slippery with wet—and down the same path we had crawled earlier. We scrambled into our sleeping bags (partly dry) in order to doze for a couple of hours. While sleeping on the hard ground, I awoke to feel my troublesome leg releasing itself in a series of heavenly ripples.

In the morning, we faced the larger challenge of finding dry tinder to light the fire—again with flint. This time success made the quail's eggs so delicious! Then, because our time was almost at an end, our leader shared with the group that she had broken some ribs just five days ago. So here was the opportunity to treat her using Myofascial Release,[14] on

---

[14] John Barnes Myofascial Release Approach is a unique form of hands-on treatment. It addresses the physical body, the emotions, the mental aspect, and the spiritual connection to our universe. During a treatment, a therapist places his or her hands at different places on the client's body, based upon what the client has said, what their physical body shows, as well as intuitive guidance. There is a deep, yet, gentle connection into the client's fascia, which is connective tissue. The fascia is the key to communication within and outside each person, and in it is stored consciousness, memory, emotion, and trauma. As a person stores things in their body—whether from physical injury, emotional trauma, or mental anguish—restrictions form, limiting movement and causing pain. Myofascial Release allows us to release the restriction, which in turn allows the trauma and emotion to be completely cleared. This leads to feeling better physically, mentally, and emotionally.

the sandbar beside the river, with some of the other women contributing energy, sage grass smudge, and warmed stones. It was a very powerful experience for us all! On this wilderness journey I discovered that I have excellent night vision.

Not once was I scared that a bear would come—because I *am* the bear.

I *can* climb, and so what if I fall?

And so, I returned from Wild Woman Weekend a much larger person with fewer fears and such deep thankfulness for my new sisters.

Wild Woman Weekend was hosted by Christina Cedar, on the banks of the Spirit River in Alberta, Canada.

—**Pearl Smith,** *RMT, practices John Barnes Myofascial Release exclusively. She has attained Expert Level as a therapist and embraces all aspects of the growth she and her clients have achieved. www.stillwatersmfr.com*

ANIMALS AS CONNECTORS

Affirmation: My body, mind, and soul rejoice, as the infinite connection I make with nature brings me closer to the divine aspect I share with all living things.

A Reflection of Time

As the dragonfly whirls,
Its vividness mesmerizes me.
Colorful memories abound,
Representative of who I am.
Illusion dissolves;
The transformation seemingly quick.
But reality demands an imperfection
To allow change.
The achievement only a minute recognition
Of completion—
A fraction of accountability dispersing into the air,
Marking the time of maturity and obscurity
To evolve—into light.

MAKING THE CONNECTION

Connectors are those animals that bring you closer to your environment or community, your family, and to yourself. Through their presence and actions, they help you to understand the need to transform your energy into the higher vibrations of unconditional love, commitment, and truth. They may also be telling you that your connection to the earth energies is off balance, and it is time to get real about your life.

Although any animal can be a connector, (the beaver in Loretta Zaluski's story, "Message Received," in the Messenger Section is an example), it is insects that most often communicate our need for connection to us.

As insects are community and family orientated, they show us how to work together for the common good of society. Every member has their job to do, and the others depend upon them to do it. The recognition that there's a time for work and a time for play indicates that balance is essential in order to succeed.

Insects are also very transparent in their growth. They go through extremely observable stages from birth to death.

If insects have shown up in your life, are you:

Connecting to the people who are important for your growth?

Doing your part environmentally? Within your family? Your community?

Moving forward in your life—or stuck in a place that no longer fits?

Working and communicating within your truth and integrity?

Having your needs met?

Honoring your commitments?

Allowing others their space?

I have always loved dragonflies, even before I was aware their presence had a spiritual meaning. They seem so elegant and surreal; their metaphysical meaning captures all of that. Masters of illusion, dragonflies symbolize reawakening to the magic and mystery of life, helping you to see a new perception as you release the old paradigm. They create awareness around your life changes and reflect the fact that you are going through a major transformation that expands your psychic vision.

Their bright colors remind us that as we mature, our true colors emerge, bringing us closer to our true essence. As creatures of air and water, the dragonfly encourages us to connect with our emotions instead of trying to block them, as well as reminding us to work within the light and remember we are never alone.

Their presence is illuminating, allowing in a vision of our own perfection and creating an opportunity to step into our own light. As they dip and dive, they bring to mind the ebb and flow of life. When they softly light on a convenient surface, I am reminded we always need to have a place to land in order to rest and rejuvenate before our next stage of awakening. Seeing a once vibrant carcass lying lifeless on the hard concrete surface of the sidewalk, I recognize the significance of leaving the physical plane to carry on elsewhere.

Dragonflies teach us a lot about life, helping us to acknowledge the spiritual stages we encounter as we progress on our path to enlightenment; showing our changing colors as we pass in and out of each other's life, sometimes on a high vibration and periodically carrying a low vibe; and integrating our experiences and pausing to balance before carrying on to the next stage. Passing through these stages of awareness, we climb until our work, done for now, pushes our light forward onto the next level and into rebirth.

These are our dragonfly days, and even though we don't always recognize the setting as perfect—it always is!

What magic and mystery of life has reawakened in a new perception for you … your dragonfly illumination?[15]

There is more than one type of connector in our animal kingdom. Any creature can help us connect to our feelings, community, and beyond. This next tale is about a cat that helped his pet parent realize that even though connection is important, so is knowing when it is time to let go.

TIGER POWER

I've had cats throughout my life but only a couple fully connected to me. Tiger was one of those cats, and he gave me comfort in my adolescent days.

When my aunt told me there were people giving some kittens away, I was so excited—I would be getting my very own kitten!

I knew as soon as I saw him that Tiger was the one I wanted. I didn't care when people said he was ugly because he had extra-long ears, which were noticeable right away. I told whoever mentioned his ears that I thought they made him look cute. He had black and brown stripes, which is why I called him Tiger, and as he grew, he grew into his ears.

Tiger loved popcorn twists, and I would buy a bag whenever I had money and we would share it. We'd sit on the outdoor steps quietly eating our snack and enjoying the weather. We were always together until he went tomcatting, and I went adolescent.

---

[15]   An excerpt from a blog I wrote and posted on my website—
www.expecttobeempowered.com in 2013.

We lived in the Riverdale area of Edmonton, Alberta, for about three years and moved to a few different houses while there. Tiger automatically knew we had moved and would come to his new home on his own.

One day he came home all beat up. His mouth was bloody and so badly ripped up that it was hanging. I wanted to take him to the vet, but I didn't know where to find one and, besides, we were poor. So, I bandaged him up and kept him home for a couple of weeks. I felt guilty for a long time because I couldn't give him the real care he needed. Once he was healing well, I let him go out again. I now called him Tiger Power because his mouth had healed with minimal scars.

After a couple of years we moved to the Cromdale area of Edmonton. I brought Tiger and showed him the new house. He stayed a couple of days and then went missing. My first instinct was that he went home to Riverdale. I kept hoping he would come back—but he never did. After a couple of months, I was satisfied that he had gone back to Riverdale because that was his home.

After the winter passed, I decided to take a bus and go into Riverdale to look for him. I started walking toward the area we had lived in last. When I was about a block away, I saw a cat. He started walking toward me. I yelled out, "Tiger, Tiger Power?" My heart beat loudly in my ears. I hoped and prayed it was him. I called him again, and he started to run toward me as I ran toward him. I grabbed him in my arms and looked at his mouth. He had the scars—it was him! I hugged him, and he rubbed his head on me. I told him I missed him a lot, but I also understood that this was his home and that I wasn't here to bring him to my home. As I looked into his eyes and he looked into mine, he purred. I hugged him some more and told him we were both grown up and have our own lives now. I was glad he was looking good and that he seemed happy. When I put him down he rubbed himself around my legs and then walked away. As I stood there looking at him, he ran across the street. I waved at him and started my walk back up the hill. I now had closure.

I didn't know it at the time, but I always took comfort that he was a survivor like me. We were two connected beings that would always be family even though we lost touch with each other.

I loved that cat!

—Julia Oh

Animals will often appear to let you know if you are on the right path in your life. They will show up to confirm your decisions, thus connecting you to the universal energy of consciousness and thanking you for your part in it.

My Fascination with Crows

It was in June of 2009 that I had this amazing encounter.

I'm basically a *white* woman, but at one time I was married to an Ojibwa man. We had four children together—three daughters and one son.

My present husband and I have been in the practice of spending up to three months in the South Padre Island/South Texas area (between late November and early March) since 2003. During late February 2008, I was on my daily, early morning beach visit when I heard a voice say, "You should do a tobacco ceremony before you leave." I didn't know where that had come from and so basically ignored it. But the next morning, the same message came to me when I was once again on the beach. I phoned my eldest daughter, who lived in Thunder Bay, Ontario (she had been following her native ways for a few years at that time), and told her what had happened.

She was quite interested in my whole experience, which included my deep interest in picking up little shells with holes in them (my *holey/holy* shells) for the past few days, as well as this strange message. She said that she was actually in the Kenora, Ontario, area with a group of elders and others who were praying for people to be called into the native Midewin society. And strange as it sounded—I seemed to have gotten the *call* from over 3,000 miles away. I continued my *holey/holy* shell collection until leaving for Canada and noted that I had a total of thirty-nine of these shells. I certainly didn't understand the significance of that number at the time.

Anyway, I went with my daughter to the *summer ceremonies* in June 2008 in the Kenora area. As we drove down the road to the *pow-wow* grounds, I noticed a barely visible sign in the bush that said, *You are entering Iskutewisakaygun, Independent First Nation #39*. Wow! Real confirmation (with the number 39) of being *called* to this particular spot in the universe! Later that day, I received my special *miigis* shell (a little shell native to Fiji, with a tiny hole in it—another confirmation) along with my first instructions to *join* this special society.

A little later, while helping with the work of setting up lodges, etc., my rings slipped off my finger. After looking for quite a while, we found two of them, but my grandmother's wedding ring from 1901 was still missing. Earlier in the day, we'd seen a family of crows encouraging their *babies* to fly. Someone said that crows like shiny things, and they may have picked up my ring. The next morning as my daughter and I were leaving the motel, there were a pair of crows that seemed to be watching us. I had a sandwich packed for lunch—so I decided to break a couple of pieces off it and put them on the ground. I spoke to the crows and, amazingly enough, each came and took a piece! Then I said: "Okay, now I'd like my ring back. It's just a shiny object to you, but it's very special to me." When we got back to the grounds, a few of us looked for the ring again, and—all of a sudden—there it was! I believe the crows and I understood each other very well. And so began my fascination and love for crows.

One of the initiation stipulations was to come to the *winter ceremonies* around Christmas to receive further instructions. I knew I'd be in south Texas at the time and wondered about how I would actually attend.

But, when the time came in December, I was physically and financially able to fly all the way from south Texas, to Winnipeg, Manitoba, and drive from there to Kenora—in the midst of a raging snow storm—and get the necessary instructions to continue on toward my initiation. The *elder* was very impressed, because there were other candidates living around Winnipeg who didn't make it to the ceremonies, using the inclement weather as an excuse. Bonus points for the lone *white* candidate!

Then came June and time for the actual ceremonies. My initiation actually happened on June 19th—which was the anniversary of my parents' wedding day in 1935. I've learned that there are no coincidences—they're just God's way of remaining anonymous!

Anyway, I had rented a little nearby cottage for the few days I'd be there; I needed a place with a little stove so I could cook my food that was part of the initiation *deal*. The day before the ceremony, while we were receiving instructions, a man drove up on a motorcycle and said, "I hear you're initiating a white woman?" The elder simply said it was a way of life available to everyone, but I was quite afraid by this incident. I certainly didn't want to be the cause of any trouble for this great bunch of people.

Anyway, I partially prepared the food later that day and got things ready for the next day. I had to be on the grounds before 7:00 a.m.— my cottage was only a few miles away—and I was up and ready to go before 6:00 a.m. As I got to the road off the highway, the first thing I noticed were three or four deer playfully jumping back and forth across the road. Then—at a small clearing—an *amazing* sight! In an instant, four crows came up from the ground together, right in front of my car, in a twirling/swirling formation, and each one flew off in a different direction. Even a video camera couldn't have caught this—it happened so quickly! And then, as I got a little farther down the road, there was a *huge* turtle just sitting there, seemingly watching me go by. The elder had told me that I had a turtle where I go *in the south* (Texas) who has been helping me. And there it was—come to say *congratulations* to me!

The ceremony was very special—I started crying as soon as the elder started praying. And everyone said my food was delicious. It was an all-around beautiful experience!

That night, I had a dream about a *loving man* whom I didn't recognize— he held my hand, and kissed me, and said, "I know you—I was there when you were born!" Wow! Was that God? Or Jesus? It didn't really matter. The fact is that my Creator has shown me that He's in my life and apparently wanted me to take part in and somehow be connected with the native or aboriginal section of humankind.

I still continue this journey—one day at a time—going wherever I seem to be led. And the crows and I still exchange messages and/or food occasionally!

—**Helaine Dufoe** *was born in Thunder Bay, Ontario, but lived from 1967 onward in Sudbury, Ontario. She studied classical piano at an early age; music ended up filling in a lot of her life's emptiness. After overcoming alcohol addiction, her life became very spiritual. This story is just one of the amazing experiences that she enjoyed.*

The smallest things can often claim your attention for the longest period of time. Time can even become nonexistent as you become captivated in examining life's treasures. One woman's day became a classroom as she connected with one of God's fascinating creatures.

Carrie had sent me this story, which happened several years ago, about a year ago and then, just recently, her bumblebee epic that occurred not long ago. If you enjoyed Carrie's story, "Bumblebee ER," you will find the following story just as enlightening.

EVERY PRECIOUS LIVING THING

One hot summer day, my mom and I decided to take a late afternoon drive to a local beach called Point Michaud, near St. Peter's, on Cape Breton Island, Nova Scotia. This beach is locally known for excellent surfing waves, the walk down the long expanse of sandy beach, and, of course, the numerous sand dollars scattered along its shoreline. Thunderous sounds of crashing waves, tidal designs carved into the sparkling sand, calls of local birds scavenging for quick meals, tall blades of wispy grass dancing in the wind, and the fresh smell and taste of the salty air … make this beautiful place a feast for one's senses.

I have to say that I turn into a different person the nearer I get to any beach, and this day was no different. Once there, the child in my adult body immediately starts scanning every crevice the beach has to offer. With empty pockets (I know too soon will be filled), my eyes dart left and right, searching for a treasured find that will soon be all mine. Interest is peaked and senses are alert for the excitement, once you find what you didn't even know you were looking for.

Beachcombing brings me back to the feelings I experienced as a child when opening up wrapped presents. Not knowing what was in each one, yet I was almost more excited ripping it apart than I was of finding the actual present inside. The anticipation was exhilarating. So too are the feelings I get scavenging the shoreline for the beach presents that make me feel like I find pirates' gold every time.

So there we were, Ma and I, enjoying the views and scanning the shoreline. We were walking, talking, and showing each other *cool finds* from shells, rocks, sand dollars, and interesting sand formations. The indecisiveness of *Is this the one?*, and having only limited pocket space, is always such fun. So is not knowing what is up ahead that could be bigger, better, and would trump anything you might have decided upon earlier, that you know you will have to carry *all the way back to the car.*

What was that? I thought as my eyes darted quickly to the left. Something was rolling in the rippling waves on the shoreline. You know, the white foamy suds the final waves make when they reach their way up the sand. That's where it was, rolling back and forth as the waves continued to draw in and out. It was about the size of a large, cut up, baby carrot, the ones that you get in those little bags at the grocery store. Yet, it wasn't super small or else I wouldn't have caught it out of the corner of my eye.

Bending over to pick up what I thought was a very cool looking rock, shell, or piece of driftwood, I couldn't believe what I was seeing. It was a *grasshopper*, rolling back and forth in the surf, unable to get enough leverage to get onto lifesaving, firm ground. He was a *goner* for sure, I thought. That he was drowning, I had no doubt.

Now for all those people who upon reading this would say, "It's a grasshopper. What's the big deal?" Well, for me, it was the closest time I have ever come to *saving a life* and the most spiritual Zen feeling of peace, from start to finish, that I have ever felt in my entire life. Time seemed to stand still for me at that moment. What would transpire over the next hour and a half would for some, seem silly. For me, it was a moment in time shared with a living, breathing creature that almost died, yet got a second lease on life. Call it luck or divine guidance—you tell me. I believe it was the latter, so I figured I would share this experience with others who might appreciate it. For those who might not understand the significance of this event, that I was blessed to have experienced, I hope you someday find something that makes you feel the way I did during my brief encounter with the Point Michaud grasshopper.

So let's get back to visualizing this large, *cut up, baby carrot-looking thing* rolling in the waves. As I picked it up, to my surprise—like I said—it was a real living grasshopper. I have never, ever seen one this big, and he wasn't looking good either. I honestly thought he was dead. In an instant he was in my hand, and I could see every part of him/her. I kept calling it *him*, so let's go with that. Well, as soon as he was out of the water and lying sideways in my hand, he immediately vomited all the saltwater that he had obviously swallowed. Now, in grasshopper size, this was obviously not a lot. However, to see a living thing that small vomit in your hand after almost drowning was something else to be seen. I literally got him out and just in time, it appeared.

Now again, many might think, "That is gross." However, imagine the adrenaline you would have after seeing a person or larger animal come back from near drowning and take its first breath. It is not something a person sees every day, let alone having it happen to an insect right in your hand. I was excited for the dear little thing—that he was actually alive. Grasshoppers aren't my thing for sure, but how could someone not be moved by watching that?

Well, Mr. Grasshopper obviously was *exhausted* because he just lay in my hand for what seemed like a very long time. He had no interest in hopping away like their normal instinct is. He had just been *snatched from the depths of the shallow tide water,* and he obviously needed to regroup and rest, no matter where he was. He wasn't moving much yet at all, and I was quite satisfied watching this little guy get his strength back. Plus—where did I have to be? I was at the beach and in no hurry. Time always stands still at the beach, right?

So I studied him intently, while he lay still in my hand, and it was neat to see him that close. By this time, Ma decided to keep walking up the beach, as she knew I was obviously too engrossed in this grasshopper rescue and was staying put with him. I could so clearly see his antennae, big eyes, mouth parts, wings, abdomen, thorax, three pairs of legs—it all came rushing back from my high school biology days learning about animal/insect parts. However, it was way cooler seeing one up close and personal, in my hand, after such a tough ordeal that he had just had. No wonder he appeared to be resting and not in a rush to get away.

After more time had passed, he vomited a little more. He then started to rouse and move his little legs ever so slightly. Now, as anyone can attest to the effect of saltwater on your body, it is sticky on your skin once it starts drying. Well, it appeared no different for this little grasshopper. He slowly started to move his legs back and forth (almost like when you put grease on something that is having trouble moving). He was getting his body parts going again too. He didn't appear to have any broken legs, which I can't imagine how he didn't, after tumbling like he did in the surf against all the little pebbles—they would be like boulders to us in comparison to his body size. However, I watched in anticipation as he moved every one of them in and out, up and down, numerous times.

Mr. Grasshopper was still in the palm of my hand. Although he had managed to get himself upright, he was still in no hurry to leave the comfort of my solid hand. Next, he decided to clean off his eyes because as anyone who has gotten salt water in their eyes knows, it is irritating and itchy. It was then I noticed an interesting feature on his body. I hadn't realized that grasshoppers have claw-type hands (almost like that of a sloth, if you have ever seen their hands). It is almost like when a person is opening and closing their hands, making the sign referring to people who talk too much (blah, blah, blah). So, just as a cat preens and grooms itself, so too did this little grasshopper get down to doing the same type of job on himself from head to toe—as the saying goes. He put his claws in his mouth, each time, before appearing to rub both of his eyes, then forehead area and each antenna. He switched back and forth to do each leg individually and any and every body part he could wet from his mouth and rub on his body, appearing to get the saltwater off of him no matter how long it took.

Well, I was just so engrossed in watching this whole thing that I hadn't realized how far Ma had walked ahead of me. You could hardly see her anymore, as it is such a long beach. However, I really was more interested in the grasshopper's *well-being*, so I decided to stay put, be his *human lighthouse after his stormy seas event* and let him take all the time he wanted to do his thing. After he took great care grooming himself, he decided to venture out a little farther on my hand. He started to crawl up the side of my hand, and I slowly turned it over as he crawled to the backside of my hand. He was being very careful and going very slowly. You really could feel him hanging on tightly (as tight as grasshoppers can do, I guess, as I have never had one cling to me like that before).

It was a beautiful, sunny afternoon that day. I know everyone has experienced the warmth of the sun's rays on their body as they lie on the ground or sit outside on a summer day. Well, I don't think anyone appreciated it more than this little grasshopper did that day. He seemed to decide to sunbathe for as long as he wanted to, on the back of my hand, with no regard to it being attached to a human. I was still so enthralled with watching him that he could have stayed there for as long as he wanted. I wasn't going anywhere. I was in total bliss. That might be hard for people to believe when talking about a grasshopper, but nonetheless, I was as content as I could be, *living in the moment*. What is a better feeling than that? Then I heard Ma's voice saying, "Have you been here this whole time? Are you still dealing with that grasshopper?" Obviously she did not get what a dramatic event it had turned out to be, so I tried to tell her all about it. I guess you had to be there, and it turned out she didn't feel the same excitement I did about the whole grasshopper near-death experience. I explained I was going to try to put him down over by the grass in a little bit, so she just kept walking back down the beach in the direction of the car again. We were in no rush, and Ma enjoys walking on the beach anyway. She said to take my time. I thought, *That's good, because I seem to be on grasshopper time, and he's in no rush to leave my secure hand just yet*. He was managing to walk around more on my fingers, and I just kept turning my hand back and forth, over and over, but he had no intention of jumping off. I guess he was just testing out his working legs some more.

All the while, when I could, I took photos with the other hand. I knew I wanted to have proof of this interaction and to look back on this wonderful experience in the future. I decided to walk around more on the beach giving him plenty of opportunity to jump off if he wanted. Nope. He was along for the ride. I knew I couldn't take him home. *What do grasshoppers eat? How long do they live?* were a few questions that popped into my head. Yet, he deserved to live in the wild, and I didn't feel right taking him from there, regardless. He seemed much better by then. He just didn't want to leave my hand. It was too funny. It was like the puppy or kitten that follows you home. Only it was a grasshopper. Not quite the pet I wanted, but it was funny to think about him staying on me for so long.

I decided to scan around for a good place to eventually put him. That way he could take all the time he wanted to finish recouping, and I could head down the beach with Ma. By this time Ma was back up to me again. I knew she wanted to go, as it was getting later in the day. She had walked the whole beach up and back and then part way up again to get back to me. I hadn't moved from this spot since I first found Mr. Grasshopper, so I wasn't really being much company. Plus, we had to drive about an hour to get home, and we wanted to do it before dark.

So, I found a piece of driftwood that was sturdy enough to push into the sand so he could sit on top of it. It was so strange to me, with all my moving around and bending over to fix the driftwood, that he didn't jump off of my hand. I really couldn't believe it, to be honest. Ma couldn't believe it either, watching him walk on my hand, knowing how long ago I had originally picked him up out of the surf. That was a long time, for sure. So I put him on the driftwood and walked away. I figured I'd stay close by just to check and see if he stayed there or hopped off it. Well, he did hop off the driftwood, but he didn't hop as far as normal grasshoppers jump, so he landed in the sand. By the time I got back to him, some ants were crawling close to him, and he wasn't going anywhere really. Plus, he had just been rolled around in salt water, and you know how sand gets everywhere. He was *salty, sandy, and waterlogged* for sure. He needed a good place to really dry out for longer, if he was going to have any chance at his new lease on life.

Well, the thought of seeing the ants coming for him freaked me out. I thought, *We didn't go through all this, Mr. Grasshopper, for you to be eaten by the ants and carried off to their ant hill.* Not on my watch! I would have to find him a better place to stay. Ma was helping at this point and taking photos, as I really had invested a lot of time and energy into this grasshopper, and I was determined to give him every opportunity to live. So, I went over to the tall grass that bordered the whole beach. The grass was really tall compared to him. I put the driftwood over there in the sand and put him on it again. I stood close by on ant duty and watched him further. He did eventually jump onto a long blade of grass and started crawling upward. That was enough proof to me that he would be all right.

In that good-bye moment with Mr. Point Michaud Grasshopper, I bid him adieu and wished him lots of luck in his saved life (however long that would be). I came to find out later that grasshoppers have a lifespan of about a year including being an egg, nymph, and adult. It seems adults can live for three to five months, depending on environmental conditions. Regardless of how long that grasshopper had left to live, he was spared a drowning death when I found him. I found myself smiling from ear to ear as I left that grasshopper clinging to the tall grass waving in the breeze, where he should have been, in my opinion, not in the ocean. Yet, as I left, I was filled with raw emotion as well. Whether anyone can ever fully understand what I felt that day doesn't really matter much to me. All I know is that I saved a life. It wasn't a large life, but it left an imprint on my own life, in a very large way. Every time I am at a beach, I think of that experience with Mr. Grasshopper. I am reminded how fragile life really is and how at any moment it can be extinguished, whether we are ready for it or not. Sometimes we are given opportunities or are put in a certain person's/animal's path for reasons we will never really know. I truly believe I was taught many great lessons that day at Point Michaud Beach. "Life is not measured by the breaths we take, but by the moments that take our breath away,"[16] as the saying goes. We need to enjoy the little things in life more. I definitely did that

---

[16] The original author of this quote is unknown, although it has been credited to a few people from Eleanor Roosevelt to Maya Angelou.

the day I met Mr. Grasshopper. That day at the beach was one of the best moments of my life, and those memories and photos, in my mind, will last forever. It was such a peaceful moment from beginning to end.

Another lesson is that kindness comes back to you a thousand fold. That day I was true to who I feel I am as a person. I was kind and compassionate to a living creature, which ended up being a significant memory in the big scheme of my life. I feel blessed that I am the kind of person who sees the value in helping and doing for others, even something as small as a grasshopper (sorry to the ants, as that would have been the meal of the century, but friends don't let friends get eaten—especially after they've nearly drowned). I have also had many kindnesses shown to me over the years, and I believe what goes around comes around. I truly believe you reap what you sow and get back what you give.

Finally, this experience reminds me of the starfish story where the little child is throwing back the starfish, that the waves cast onto the beach, so they would not die.[17] The adult doesn't see why the child is doing it because there were so many, and they could not all be saved. The reason he was doing it, the child says, is that if he made a difference to that one starfish that he threw back, then that was all that mattered. I feel that way about Mr. Grasshopper. What mattered was that I saw a need, I stopped what I was doing in my daily life, and I showed love. To the world I am only one person, but to that living creature I saved that day, I was the world. I grew as a better person having had that experience with such a small, yet still important, life of a grasshopper.

Years later, I was on another beach while traveling the Cabot Trail in Cape Breton. I always do think of that day with Mr. Grasshopper, and it causes my heart to smile. Well, this day in particular, I caught a glimpse of a cool looking piece of driftwood mixed among a bunch of rocks. When I bent down to pick it up, I actually laughed out loud.

---

[17]   Original author of this well-known story is Loren Eisley.

When what to my wondering eyes should appear, but driftwood in the shape of a grasshopper, my dear. I still have it hung on my deck to this day to remind me of all the lessons I learned from my little insect friend.

I decided to look up the meaning behind a grasshopper's appearance. It seems if you cross paths with a grasshopper, you are being asked to jump forward, without fear, and take a leap of faith in a particular area of your life that involves great change. The changes could be about how we view ourselves: employment, relationships with others, or where we are currently living. A neat fact I found was that grasshoppers can only jump forward, *not backward or sideways.* That I didn't know. It seems that if you see a grasshopper, it is a sign that you are moving in the right direction, which is forward, with whatever you are dealing with or contemplating. The grasshopper can also be a sign for you to move ahead and trust your inner voice. It is an earthy animal that could also show up when you need to feel more grounded with more stability in your life. The grasshopper is a symbol of good luck all over the world.[18]

After reading up on the grasshopper, I truly feel I was blessed to have had this once-in-a-lifetime interaction with such an amazing little creature. Good things do come in small packages.

Love to all creatures—great and small.

—Carrie Currie

Sometimes the connections we make are subconscious until something happens that brings the memory into consciousness and connects what is going on now with an event that occurred some time ago. This was the case in this next story.

---

[18]   http://wiki.answers.com/Q/Spiritual_meaning_of_grasshoppers#slide=1
http://www.whats-your-sign.com/grasshopper-totem-and-symbolism.html

Free Spirit

In May 2008, while I was visiting my brother and sister-in-law in Cherryville, British Columbia, my friend, Hennia, my sister-in-law, Roxy, and I were doing some sightseeing in the town.

We stopped at a beautiful art studio in Cherryville called Studio 6, which is located within a private home. The owner also has horses, which she took us to see after touring her studio. I have always loved horses and rode a few times when I was younger, but really don't have much experience with them.

One of the horses we were looking at was a huge, chestnut beauty. He seemed to take a liking to me and was nibbling on my cheek, stomping his feet, and seemingly smiling at me by showing his teeth. He was doing everything he could to keep my attention and wouldn't leave me alone.

His owner was very surprised by her horse's response to me and said, "I have never seen him act like that—especially with strangers!"

About eleven months later, I bought a new truck. Something about its shiny gold color reminded me of the horse I had interacted with some months before.

When I had purple stripes painted on my truck, I once again thought of that magnificent horse and how it signified happiness, independence, strength, and power to me.

I associate my bright gold truck and its bold purple stripes with the same characteristics the horse possessed, but the sense of freedom I get while driving it stands out.

To capture that feeling, my truck is aptly named *Free Spirit* in honor of the horse that brought these qualities to my attention. I use modern horse power to get around, but the original source of this power captured my heart and my imagination.

—As told by **Bonnie Ireland,** *a certified Sound Healer, Reiki Master, and Deep Cellular Healing Level 3 Practitioner, who has also studied Quantum Touch, shiatsu, and meditation. She has been passionately involved with and dedicated to healing for over twenty years and has more recently been guided to work with animal spirit guides. Bonnie and her husband live in Grande Prairie, Alberta.*

BEYOND EXPLANATION

Affirmation: When my body, mind, and soul believe, miracles appear!

Just Believe

When I open my eyes to the unknown,
I create knowledge beyond that I can conceive.
Who's to say it's not been there all along,
Just waiting for me to believe?

I create my life around knowledge I understand,
Not exposing myself to what I'm unable to perceive.
Who's to say it's not been there all along,
Until I open up to believe?

I accept that which I can see
And open my arms to receive.
Who's to say it's not been there all along,
Crying for me to believe?

Allowing that which seems impossible,
Information I strive to retrieve.
Who's to say it's not been there all along,
Creating an intention to believe?

Although unexplainable to me yet,
I really have to concede
It's been there all along,
And asking me to—*just believe.*

No Explanation Necessary

Once in a while you hear a story that is so unexplainable, it appears to be divinely guided. These are the tales that capture the imagination and inspire you to be better, while forming a belief in the unknown and accepting the truth that there are things greater—beyond any control you think you may have.

These stories can bring you to tears or cause you to rethink everything you thought you knew about life. As you delve deeper into the secrets of these accounts, they reaffirm faith in the correlation between all living things.

There have been many great narratives written about cohesive relationships between animals who are assumed to be mortal enemies as well as tales of the association between man and beast—one who would usually assert their power over the other in some way, but join together for a specific purpose.

We are all here to learn; we do it in the best way we can, and that often involves carrying on our ancestral beliefs of power over another living thing. When that belief is tested, it opens our eyes, enabling us to see things in a new way.

It is all part of accepting that there is a different way, an altered logic, and a new energy opening up that allows us to see everything in life, not as disempowered or less than, but equal and melding together in a continuation of life.

The next few stories will bring you a new awareness of the energy shift coming in, guiding you away from the old antiquities of thinking, and helping you embrace a new understanding of the dynamics of connecting fully to the energies of animals and nature.

When I was very young, not much more than a toddler, I followed my dad out to the barnyard. He was unaware that I was behind him until he heard a noise and turned around. What he saw then, he remembered for the rest of his life, and he relayed this incident to me many years after it had occurred.

We raised steers at the time of this event, and although fairly tame, they apparently weren't used to seeing a tiny human in the corral with them. The sound he heard that made dad turn around was me, crying. I was on the ground, my tiny body being held in place by a steer's head, its wild eyes boring into my frightened ones, with its assassin horns spearing the ground on either side of me. Dad rushed over and managed to pull me out of harm's way, but I was fairly safe where I was, the steer being imprisoned by his own horns as they held him fast to the ground.

The reason I am telling you this story is that it emphasizes how fragile life can be. If that steer or I had moved an inch or two either way, you would probably not be reading these words right now.

There is such a feeling of being protected when stories such as the above or those that are related here below are told. It is times like this that make us stop and believe that a power greater than we understand is at work in our lives.

Rescue stories involving dogs are not uncommon, and we hear these stories of sacrifice by our canine friends frequently. The following tale is a bit more unusual and shows us that our welfare is looked after in more ways than we think.

SEALED AND DELIVERED

A friend's daughter was flying to Vancouver for a job interview and met a woman who relayed this amazing story about her son.

Her son, one of twins, was twenty years old when he jumped off the iron bridge located in Vancouver, British Columbia, Canada. Although unconscious, he felt himself being pulled out of the water by what he thought was a person, but when he woke up, he was surprised to see there was a seal sitting beside him. The seal stayed with him and didn't leave his side until help showed up.

Now, many years later, this man has a family, is doing well, and is extremely grateful to his exceptional rescuer.

Once in a while, a person comes along who just seems to have a way with animals that many of us don't understand. Our perception is usually shaded by events and beliefs that keep us in fear, so unique stories such as the next one cause us to stop and reevaluate everything we thought we knew.

IF I COULD TALK TO THE ANIMALS

Some people just seem to be able to communicate with animals. My friend, Stan Peacock, is one such person.

In the 1980s, there were a few years that the Alberta government allowed live capture of deer, elk, and moose to be raised in domestic farm operations. During that time, Stan developed a one-way gate that would allow deer to enter a pen to get a free dinner, but they could not get out of the pen once they were in.

When two moose wandered into one of Stan's pens, he put them in the feedlot he had for his 800-head cow operation. The moose settled right down and accepted his offering of fodder and feed.

One of the moose was a bull who looked to be about two years old. He became a pet and would follow Stan throughout the feedlot as he fed the cattle. Stan named him Harvey, and he would follow Stan right up to the gate and then return to mingle with the cattle. He was nonassertive to other family members, but Stan was the only one Harvey would follow.

On one occasion, Stan was gone and his son fed the cattle. He did not fasten the gate properly, and when he finished the chores, he noticed the gate was ajar and Harvey was gone.

Over the next four months, there were several instances when moose tracks were found along the fence line, but Harvey was never seen.

One day, a neighbor dropped in for a visit and said he had seen a moose in a pasture one-half mile west of the farm and wondered if maybe it was Harvey.

Stan had really liked that moose, so he hiked in the direction the neighbor had indicated. He called out to Harvey as he walked and initially got no response—until suddenly he heard a bellow and a moose came out of some bush charging directly at Stan. Whether this moose was Harvey or not, Stan was concerned to have a 1,500-pound bull charging directly at him.

Knowing there was no sense running, Stan stood still and focused his attention on the moose, watching as it rushed full speed toward him. The moose stopped dead, several feet away from Stan, and just stood there as Stan talked to him as if he were Harvey.

After talking a while, Stan decided that if this creature was Harvey, he would follow him home, so he set off, and yes ... the moose followed like a puppy dog. Stan decided to offer a second test as they approached a fence. The nearest gate was one-half mile away, so Stan crawled through the fence and continued walking. The moose took the fence in a single jump and continued following his friend.

When they got to the farmstead, the moose followed Stan as he wound his way through the machinery and over to the feedlot. There Stan opened the gate and Harvey walked into the corral.

The next day they resumed their routine of feeding the cattle.

I think Stan has a special sensitivity for animals and communicates with them on a deeper level than most of us.

And what happened to Harvey? The Zoological Society in Tokyo negotiated with Stan for his pet, and Harvey went to a good home.

—**Owen Stanford** *lives in Fairview, Alberta, and earned a B.Com from the University of Calgary, becoming a Certified General Accountant while working at Revenue Canada. He switched to teaching business in the college system and loved that for twenty-six years, retiring three years ago. He and his wife, Betty, have five children. The man who had this experience is Stan Peacock. He has a large farm and a cow calf operation near High Prairie, Alberta.*

The following anecdote will have you believing not only in miracles, but will give you pause to consider what exactly links us all together— not just human connection, but our relationship to all things. To what lengths will the animals in our life go to show us their love for us? This story of Ariane and Gringo will probably not answer your questions but inspire you to ask many more.

A LOVING SACRIFICE

I would like to dedicate this story to my granddaughter, Ariane, and my dog, Gringo, my border collie that I love and miss so very much. I am a French-speaking person, and I would like to share my story to inspire faith, hope, and miracles in people.

On September 13, 2010, my granddaughter, Ariane,[19] ten years old at the time, was diagnosed with a brain cancer so rare, the WHO[20] group gave it the name *Papillary Tumor of the Pineal Gland* in 2007. At that time, seventy people in the world had this type of cancer. Ariane is one in a billion—the first in Canada and the youngest person to have been diagnosed. She needed emergency surgery to place a shunt into her brain to relieve the pressure; otherwise she would have died.

I was babysitting my son's youngest daughter, Joliane, eighteen months old at the time. When my son arrived from the hospital to pick up Joliane, he had tears in his eyes. I asked him what was wrong. He told me that the neurosurgeon had said Ariane possibly had some metastasis in her cervical and lumbar spine. We were just devastated. My son and I started crying—then I told him not to worry as I had good vibes and a strong faith that all would be well.

After my son left with the kids (Joliane and his two older boys), I cried some more; I could not believe what was happening to my granddaughter, Ariane—to my family!

My dog, Gringo, knew something was wrong because he stared at me the whole time my son was talking to me about Ariane. He knew we were very upset, and when I sat down on the couch, he came and sat beside me, trying to console me and get my attention by giving me his

---

[19]   If you google Ariane Delome, you will see what a miracle she truly is. She is known as the Singing Girl at CHEO (Children's Hospital of Eastern Ontario), and there were many articles written about her. A lot of inspiring things happened to my granddaughter, Ariane. During her surgeries she saw angels, light, and a lot more. She wrote a song called, "Bye, Bye, Bad Guy," to help others not fear cancer, and she would like to write a book one day too.

[20]   World Health Organization, an agency of the United Nations, headquartered in Geneva, Switzerland, who are concerned about international public health.

paw. It made me smile. I got close to his face and kissed his forehead. I was still upset, and he knew that, but his presence gave me a little comfort. I could feel strong vibes coming from him telling me that it was impossible that my granddaughter would die. I became much more positive and felt so much peace and faith—like you wouldn't believe!

Two days later, Ariane needed a second surgery to remove as much of her brain tumor as possible. Doctors were able to remove a small portion and drain the cysts around the tumor to relieve the pressure on her brain. For her third surgery, she would be transferred to the SickKids Hospital in Toronto when she stabilized.

One night she developed so much pain in her head that she was rushed to the intensive care unit in critical condition. My son called me during the night to say that he needed me to drive him to the hospital, because my daughter-in-law had the car, and Ariane was in such serious condition that they thought they might have to do another emergency surgery to relieve the pressure on her brain to save her.

When I went to see her, Ariane was comatose in ICU. I grabbed her hand and told her I needed her to come back. I sent her positive vibes, light, angels, and prayers. My son, daughter-in-law, and I did a rotation throughout the night in ICU. I don't remember what time it was on my turn when she said, "Hello Mamie,"—which means *grandmother*. I cried and held her hands, then went and got my son and daughter-in-law. We were all so happy!

The MRI showed that Ariane still had lesions on her cervical and lumbar spine. I remember crying one night because we kept getting bad news regarding her cervical and lumbar spine lesions. I was sitting at my kitchen table with an angel statue holding a tea candle and sending positives vibes, angel's light, and prayers to Ariane, with my dog, Gringo, at my feet just staring at me. When I bent down to greet him, he licked me on the cheek. The tears were running down my face, and I knew he could feel my pain.

The next day I was babysitting Joliane again. It was a Friday—something I will always remember. I went to let my two dogs outside when I noticed Gringo was not moving at all. I found that weird because he loved to be outdoors. As I approached him, I noticed he couldn't move his behind. I started to cry and called my husband at work and asked him to come home because something was wrong with Gringo. He still had not moved. It was as if he were paralyzed. When my husband got home, we decided to wait and see if he would get better in a few hours. Well, a few hours passed, and he was still the same. We then took him to the vet—he was still paralyzed, but had no pain. We were told Gringo had to go to Saint-Hyacynthe in Quebec for an MRI and surgery. That meant I had to be out of town while my granddaughter was still not stable and was still in ICU waiting to be transferred to Toronto and—not only that—my husband was also leaving for Halifax for work for a week. The vet told us he was not sure if Gringo would ever walk again, even with the surgery, and suggested that maybe we could just put a kind of wagon on his hip. I could not make the decision as I knew Gringo loved to run after his ball, and we have five levels of stairs in our house.

My husband told me to wait in the car. While waiting, I started to cry so hard that I was out of breath. I then screamed, "Please, I want you to take my dog. Please, God and angels, take Ariane's cancer and cervical and lumbar lesions with Gringo. Please leave Ariane with us—she's so young—don't take her too!"

We ended up having to put Gringo to sleep. It was so sad.

The following week, Ariane was transferred to Toronto SickKids Hospital for her third surgery; it went as well as planned. We returned to Ottawa five days after the surgery, where she had an MRI. The neurosurgeon could not believe how fast Ariane had recuperated. Ninety-five percent of her tumor was gone, and the lesions on her cervical and lumbar had decreased a lot, but she still needed thirty sessions of radiation therapy.

On January 14, 2014, my son told me that the last MRI that had been done a few weeks ago on Ariane showed no more traces of cervical and lumbar spinal lesions.

When Ariane found out about the passing of Gringo, she cried. I told her how I had asked the angels and God to let Gringo take her cancer and cervical and lumbar spine lesions.

She says that Gringo saved her life by sacrificing his life for her.

Gringo did not have any signs or symptoms of having any problems with his back or legs the week prior to his death; he had been playing and jumping and was pain free. Gringo was only five years old, and we were blessed to have him in our life. Today it is still a mystery to our family about what happened to him when he suddenly became paralyzed.

Deep inside, I feel he was in our family for a reason, and that reason was Ariane. I am a very positive person who believes in God and angels, and I believe in miracles! Because Ariane is one!

—**Helene Gamache**

Sometimes things happen that force us to reevaluate our priorities or actions. Such is the case in the following tale. It seemed a usual day that turned out to have a totally unexpected outcome and changed a life.

WHY?

One fall day, several years ago, I was guiding for a nonlocal hunter to our area around Fairview, Alberta. Although I am not a hunter myself, I have never judged anyone else for chasing game.

As we proceeded into the bush, I spotted a black bear. He did not appear to be overly big, but was formidable, as bears can be. Carefully pointing his bow and arrow, the hunter aimed and hit the bear, wounding it. The frightened bear then turned and ran further into the bush.

Knowing it was badly injured by the amount of blood that was coming from the wound, I followed the bear into a clearing where it stood up and looked straight at me. It looked dazed and confused and was in a lot of pain. Then, time seemed to stand still as, wordlessly, we shared a connection that was beyond anything I have ever experienced before or since, as we communicated back and forth. Not a syllable was uttered between this great beast and myself, but … I heard the word as clearly as if it had been spoken aloud. The energy of that one word had more impact on me than one hundred words ever could. That one small, three-letter word we shared that day in the bush made me rethink life as I knew it and question the balance of power many believe man has over nature.

As the word *Why?* was emitted in the frosty air of that autumn morning, I was only aware of the stillness around me. The explosion within my heart seemed as loud as the gunshot I heard from behind me, as the bear was released from the pain knifing through his physical body, by the hunter.

The impact of that entire incident is something that I thought about often over the next few years. Although a gut-wrenching experience and definitely the last time I will ever participate in a hunt in any way, I also feel I was given a great gift, by being let in on an ancient secret that few would ever know.

The communication I shared with the bear that day has given me a glimpse into the doorway of the animal kingdom and, with it, the realization that we are not so different—it is only our illusion of power that makes us think so.

—As told by **Keith Lyons** *who lives in Fairview, Alberta. Keith is a farmer and local business owner.*

ENCOUNTERS

Affirmation: My body, mind, and soul recognize the value of sharing my life with animals and how every aspect of my life's journey is improved by their presence.

No Barriers

Not a day goes by that I am alone;
My heart guides me to where animals roam.
They speak in a way I can't explain,
But I recognize the language all the same.

As I listen to the guidance they freely give,
I see the credence they impart me to live.
Their power, beyond compare,
Conveys wisdom they freely share.

Their messages, not to be ignored;
Enlightenment—the reward.
This gift of connection blesses me
With knowledge beyond what I can see.

I need not understand everything,
Just accept what they bring
As they offer insight to embrace,
Guiding gently with ease and grace.

Not a day goes by that I am alone;
My heart guides me to where animals roam.
They speak in a way I can't explain,
But I recognize the language all the same.

MEANINGFUL INTERACTIONS

Are the many encounters you have with animals just a meeting between species as you are busy continuing your life, or are they a reminder for you to stop and pay attention?

In order to answer this question, look at the circumstances of the interaction. Is it an everyday occurrence with your household or barnyard pet? Is it an event that is unusual in any way? Is there a question or intention you have put out to the universe?

For example, I have many squirrels and birds where I live, so I don't pay much attention to them unless a squirrel happens to get into the house or a bird hits my window, because it rarely happens.

I did have an incident with my dogs a few years ago that had me searching for answers.

The dogs are really good about doing their business far away from the house where we can't see any evidence. One day as I walked out the front door onto the deck, I noticed that one of the dogs had defecated practically right in front of the door. It was impossible to know which one, as we had three at the time, so thinking it was just an isolated incident, I cleaned it up and forgot about it.

Well, the next day it happened again—this time on the steps going down from the deck. I remember being quite angry about this and gave all three dogs a talking to. It wasn't until the episode occurred three days in a row that I clued into the idea that I was getting a message. Once I had this insight, I realized that the message I was receiving was all about boundaries. My boundaries, at the time, were not well defined about many things, and the dogs were communicating this to me by their behavior. Once I realized this, there were no more messes close to the house.

Of course, I felt bad about giving the dogs trouble and so turned that around by thanking them for their announcement.

Interactions like this, with our animal friends, happen regularly, but it is our willingness to listen to what we are being told that makes the difference for us.

The next story was a very meaningful encounter I had about a year ago. I am getting better at discerning the messages from animal encounters as being a matter of clarity for me, or as just a common interaction, and knew immediately that this contact was a timely communication.

In the afternoon of the day before I left on a cross-Canada tour promoting my first book, *Waves of Blue Light: Heal the Heart and Free the Soul*, my granddaughter, Lexi, and I decided we would go on a final horseback ride until I returned in the fall. We had barely started our ride accompanied by our three dogs, Apollo, Clyde, and Beckie, when Lexi exclaimed, "Grandma—there's a baby deer!" Not seeing it, I asked her where it was, and she turned her horse, Spencer, around, leading me back to where she had seen it. The dogs spotted it at the same time she did, scaring the fawn so badly that it stood up from the long grass where it had been hiding and ran into the bush.

The dogs, always excited for a good run, chased it. Upon hearing the human-like crying coming from the fawn as the dogs found and began mauling it, I jumped down off of my horse, Girl, and followed the disturbing sound of screaming cries. After shouting at the dogs to leave it alone, I reluctantly looked down, uncertain and afraid of what I might see. A feeling of dread overcame me when I saw the baby deer was not moving at all, and there was a smear of blood marring its beautiful, soft, brown hide.

Feeling extremely teary-eyed and swallowing the lump in my throat, I bent down and picked up this soft, gentle creature, willing it to move and show some sign of life. As I lifted it, the fawn had a resurgence of energy and began crying and kicking its long, thin, pole-like legs. What a relief I felt as I hugged this perfect baby to me.

Coming back out of the bush to where Lexi was holding the horses and watching for the doe, I showed her the struggling fawn and said, "I guess the only thing to do is bring her back to the farm and see how badly she is hurt." Giving the little deer to Lexi to hold, I climbed back onto Girl and had Lexi lift her up into my arms for the ride back home. At first the fawn seemed to struggle, but she settled down quickly and was very docile most of the time, with the occasional cry and intermittent kicking of legs.

After getting back home and seeing she was okay and that the blood was just a scratch, we locked the dogs up so we could take our precious find back to where we first spotted it, thinking that would be the best place for her mama to locate her. The ride back to the trees was quite uneventful, as by this time, the fawn had come to trust us, and even Girl going into a trot did not seem to disturb her. She was quite alert and even seemed to enjoy the ride.

After being released, the baby slipped into the trees, but we wanted to make sure she was okay. Knowing that the doe would not attempt to find her baby while we were there, we decided to take a little ride and come back in a few hours to check on the situation.

Upon our return, we saw the doe pacing the perimeter of the trees, so we thought she had been reunited with her fawn. Stopping to look at the place we had left the baby, we were unable to see any sign of it, so we figured that she had been found, hidden again, and was safely back in her mother's care.

Reflecting back on this event and intuiting my knowledge of the energy of animals and how they affect what is going on in our lives, I believe I was being given the message of combining grace, ease, and baby steps for the tour. That is certainly the formula I have followed, and it worked perfectly.

Thank you, Mama Doe, for lending me your baby and trusting it would be returned safely. I know how hard it must have been for you to let her go, because after only knowing her for a few hours, it almost broke my heart to bring her back home, even though I knew that is where she belonged.

The greatest gifts are often only given to us for a short time. Appreciate all things in your life, as you never know how long they will be yours.[21]

Often encounters are born out of a need either to understand or communicate from a deeper level. The author of this next story found some solace in her amazing communication. Her deep trust, union, and understanding of connective and universal energy enabled her to receive a healing message.

A MAGICAL MOMENT

I find it lovely that the Celtic year ends with *Samhain* (Halloween) but does not begin until solstice. This honors the space between life, death, and rebirth. After all, it is the space between the beat of a drum that defines the rhythm and the space between the in and out breath that allows us to shift our flow.

A few days ago, I received news that a friend had died on the morning of Samhain. I began to think of experiences that have given me faith in the mystery of existence beyond the physical.

---

[21]   Originally written as a blog on my website in 2013—
www.expecttobeempowered.com.

I am not one who sees ghosts, but I have felt the magic of connection between the realms. Usually it comes through the assistance of animals acting as messengers. Many signs we have been given from nature show us that the connection we have with loved ones is not lost after their body turns to ashes or becomes one with the earth.

Let me begin this story with a memory of love. I say love because that is what my dog, Daisy, was for me. She was pure love, and I could fill a novel about her virtues and silly antics. She looked like a small *Benji* from the movies and would leap up into my arms with the snap of a finger. I called her and her brother, Dickens, my little guardian angels. When we went on our walks, I would say, "Yeehaw!" as permission for them to run off and explore. She would always jump up to lightly kiss my fingers before she joined her brother. Then they would make crisscross leaps over each other's backs as they raced forward. One day after her kiss good-bye, Daisy came running out of the woods with terror in her eyes. Seconds later she was being trampled by a deranged, parasite-infected deer. I screamed and ran forward to stop the attack, but the deer paid no attention to me. When I was just a few feet away from them, I roared out like a bear; the deer looked up and ran away. But it was too late. Daisy died in my arms, and I felt my world crumple with her last breath.

They say love does not limit itself to species but is known by the depth of our connection. She had been my little guardian for over sixteen years, and although I managed to carry on, I missed her terribly. Her brother, Dik, also felt lost without her. He wore a path down in the grass and, later in the snow, to the place we had buried her. Every morning and evening he would go there to sit. In the beginning he would howl, but later he just gazed off into space.

They say time heals, but mourning is not a flat path; there are hills and valleys when processing loss. One day a few months after she had passed, I woke up feeling overwhelmed, and I cried into my pillow, "I know you are okay, Daisy, but I so wish I could look into your eyes—just one more time. I miss you so, so much." Then, feeling limp from my emotional release, I pulled myself together again and went out to Moonshine Lake with my family. It was wintertime, and I sat on a bench, under a tree, with my four-month-old daughter resting in the nook of my crossed leg, while the rest of my family skated. A man came over and sat down beside me to eat his sandwich and chat. As we chatted, a bird flew down and sat on my foot, which was crossed over my knee. The bird had the same markings as Daisy's face, and it stared up at me—totally ignoring the man beside me. I immediately felt Daisy's energy coming to me through the bird's brown eyes.

After staying there for a bit, she flew up to a nearby tree. The man was in shock. "Why was it looking at you, when *I* am the one with food?" he asked. I didn't reply, but started to doubt my senses, telling myself, *The bird was just out for a snack. Now, if it really was Daisy communicating with me, and not just a friendly bird, she would have trusted me enough to fly to my hand. Now, if that happened, it would be more meaningful.* Almost as soon as I thought the words, the bird flew down from the tree where she had been watching me and sat by my hand. She stared up at me with her beautiful brown eyes so much like Daisy's, so full of love. I felt tears of gratitude well up in my eyes. I stared back at her and whispered softly, "I love you, too." After a timeless moment, she flew off into the forest, having granted my wish for one more gaze into my little dog's eyes.

To me, this was one of my memories of the great mystery's magic. I can't say that I understand, but I am comforted none the less. I know this small experience is but one of many, and I feel honored to share my moments of magic found in the space between.

—**Christina Otterstrom-Cedar** *was known as Tina as a child and seldom spoke to people. It was animals who were her best friends. Eventually, she learned to talk and enjoy her own kind, but her connection with animals and Mama Nature remains paramount in her life. It shapes who she is as an artist, celebrant, counselor, friend, and most of all, as a mother. Indeed* *it was Daisy who taught her the ability to surrender while giving birth, and many more animals, wild and tame, guide her every day in how to become a better animal upon this earth, under this sky.*

A sensitivity to the plight of the animal kingdom when they integrate with us, within our environment, helps us to understand their need to receive help and our need to give it. No life is too unimportant to reject when a crisis develops that may be a matter of life or death. Not only does the natural world benefit, but, we, as caregivers, profit from the respect we give ourselves by being aware of the sanctity of all life.

DUCK DAYCARE

Last July 26th, I came home about 7:00 a.m. after dropping my son, Noah, off at Cadets, to see a family of seven ducklings with their mom walking up 127th Avenue in the Crystal Lake area of Grande Prairie, Alberta.

This same duck has, for the past three years, always gotten herself and her ducklings stuck in the neighbor's yard. They would find a way into the yard with the gate locked from the inside and nowhere for them to crawl under the fence. It is still a mystery as to how they got there! They would stay in the northwest corner of the yard until the neighbor and her family would herd them out of the yard and then to the sidewalk, where they would make their way up to the lake. However, this time they made their way up the sidewalk toward the lake without a detour.

I saw them as I was pulling up to my driveway and noticed there was a runt lagging behind the rest of the group. I parked my car and started to walk behind the little runt to help him catch up to the rest of the family.

This little duckling would take ten to fifteen steps, then sit down. It continued doing this all the way up the sidewalk to Lake Shore Drive, about two houses up.

Mother duck and the rest of the ducklings were now a couple of houses ahead of the runt, so I quickly made a couple of phone calls on my cell to find out if covering my hands would work to hide my scent so the mother would not abandon her baby if I picked it up.

After finding out it was best to cover up, I pulled the white sweater I was wearing down over my hands, picked the duckling up and carried it up to the top of the hill where he suddenly jumped out of my hands, much to the delight of the hungry, gray cat that appeared at that moment. Although he tried hard to get this tasty morsel for his breakfast, I was not letting that cat get this duckling, so I stomped my feet a couple of times to scare it away. I followed the duckling across the road to make sure it stayed safe from the cat and the traffic.

I picked him up again and carried him to the edge of the water and told him, "Now that I have gotten you all the way here, it is your turn to get out there and swim to your mom and siblings."

I stayed for about ten minutes, listening to the runt quacking along with his mother and siblings … he was swimming away with the others when I left.

—**Jeanette Taylor-Mac** *is an independent business woman living in Grande Prairie, Alberta. A hairdresser for twenty-three years, Jeanette owns and operates Haircraft within the city's downtown core. A loving mom to one son, Noah, Jeanette believes in living a healthy lifestyle and treating all living things with kindness.*

Sometimes it is nice to have a visitor without consciously having to understand why they dropped in. Such is the case in the next tale.

PEACEFUL PRESENCE

One beautiful night near the end of summer, I decided to join my friend, Lesley, who had been sleeping in her hammock all season, by spending the night in my tent beside her. Her hammock was hung between two trees close to the lake. I set up camp fairly close to her, without closing the fly, so that I would have a good view of the full moon, its light shining magically on the water, and to feel its energy upon my body.

At some point during the night I woke up peacefully for no apparent reason and felt the need to sit up. As I did, I was face-to-face with a mother bear and her cub, both very quietly peeking into the tent through the open fly. I could see another cub up ahead with another one just behind. After peeking, Mama Bear and her curious cub peacefully continued on their way, catching up with the cub already ahead of them.

I felt very peaceful throughout the whole encounter, which lasted only one or two minutes. After they left and I was lying down again, my left brain kicked in—and with it a hint of caution. I thought I should let Lesley know about their presence, so I called her—just in case. I said: "Lesley, there's a bear ... a really big bear," and she quietly replied back, "Oh my!"

I said: "They are moving away," and we went back to sleep. Before falling asleep, I remember feeling honored to have been graced with the bears' quiet and peaceful presence, especially on this beautiful moonlit night by majestic Lake Superior.

The next day, Lesley and I talked about the bears' visit, and she shared that she had woken up just moments before, in the same manner as I had, with this peaceful urge to sit. She recalled that she couldn't see anything and didn't want to move. She also shared that she loved how we both fell asleep so quickly after our short exchange.

To this day, neither Lesley nor I feel the need to explain or analyze this encounter, but we both feel grateful and awed to have been woken up just in time to fully experience the gentle presence of the mama bear and her triplets for a few minutes. It certainly was an honor, and one that we both still hold dear. To us, it speaks strongly to the power of acknowledging other beings, especially the ones we humans tend to fear, from a place of love and respect.

—**Catherine Courtine** *lives in Thunder Bay, Ontario, Canada, and has always felt a deep, mystical connection with nature. As a child, even though she lived in a large city in France, she realized that insects and plants were alive, and hurting them in any way didn't feel right to her. As a teenager, she began to feel the same reverence and respect toward animals, and slowly grew into a vegetarian, which she still is, thirty-three years later. She feels that we are one with nature. We use different words to name the different things our eyes see, which influence us to think there is a separation, but she does not feel any. So for her, commu**un**icating with nature is accessing our natural state of comm**un**ion or **un**ity (**un** in French means "one").*

TOTEMS AND GUIDES

Affirmation: My life is blessed by the simple acts of oneness I experience when I am guided by love.

Listen: Raven Speaks

Before Raven spoke to me,
I was afraid and in the dark;
Wanted light—didn't know how to start.
Through the shadows, I couldn't see
Before Raven spoke to me.

Before Raven spoke to me,
I held my voice, hesitant to grow;
Wanted to speak—kept the volume low.
Through the shadows, I couldn't see
Before Raven spoke to me.

Before Raven spoke to me,
I was lost, hopeless, and weak;
Wanted strength—felt too meek.
Through the shadows, I couldn't see
Before Raven spoke to me.

Before Raven spoke to me.
I drummed alone, music lost too soon;
Wanted harmony—felt out of tune.
Through the shadows, I couldn't see
Before Raven spoke to me.

Now Raven speaks to me
Of my voice, strength, music, and light within,
Showed me the magic—freed me to begin.
There are no shadows, as I see,
Now that Raven speaks to me.[22]

---

[22] First published on page 111 of Waves of Blue Light: Heal the Heart and Free the Soul (2011) M.J. Domet

ANIMAL GUIDE COMMUNICATION

Animal guides are here to help us on our physical journey. Their presence reminds us of our frailties and our strengths. The guides ask us to embrace their company in order to reflect the qualities they have back to ourselves, so we can understand what attributes we possess in order to cope with our experiences.

Our guides make their presence known to us in several ways. They may appear physically, if they are native to our area. Sometimes a physical appearance can just be a physical appearance if the animal is a common one. It is the unusual that is to be paid attention to. This may occur in various ways, such as the animal appearing in large numbers in a group or showing up more frequently than usual. It may also appear in an unusual way for that animal or in an odd place.

If your totem is not native to where you live, you may see a picture of it in a magazine, on TV, or even a statue of it all in the same day. Again, be aware of the uniqueness of its presence.

Our guides also can appear to us in our dreams or during meditation. They can show up during a card reading or through an intuitive energy session. Often, if you feel a brushing sensation along your legs, or a sudden pressure as if something has jumped into your lap or onto your shoulder, your guide is making itself known!

Now, there are animals that appear occasionally with a timely message, who are not necessarily your main totem animal, but are still spirit guides. Generally your totem or main guide has been with you since childhood and exhibits many of the same traits you carry. They are with you much the same as an angelic spirit guide is—as an energetic helper to lead you to the appropriate choices for your human journey in this lifetime. As a guide, they cannot tell you what to do, but can help you ascertain what is in your highest good. Once you have determined who your helper(s) are, it is essential to study their traits in order to get to know your strengths. A good resource is Steven Farmer's *Animal Spirit Guides* book. It is very easy to read in order to identify the traits you have in common with your totem animal.

You may have only one primary guide and a few secondary guides who come in quite often. Your lesser guides hold characteristics that are very close to your own, but not as perfect a match as your main guide. I caution you to not dismiss an animal totem you feel is not your ideal match—yet. I say *yet*, because the traits of your guide you think you don't possess are within your potential to reach.

All animals have amazing characteristics, whether that animal comes in the form of a mouse, a beetle, a pigeon, or a lion. We are often so quick to judge without looking at facts. It doesn't matter if your guide is an ant or a bison, just as it is of no importance whether your skin is white, black, or purple—that is just the exterior.

A client of mine was quite disappointed when I told him his totem animal was a chickadee. His teasing reply was, "A chickadee! I was hoping it would be something more manly." One of the chickadee's traits is that of a *fearless warrior* (Narayan Singh, *Animal Activities: A Shaman's Handbook—Their Psychosymbolic Meanings*) because it courageously protects what is important to it. What, I ask you, is more manly than that? It is important to put judgments aside as you work with your guide, otherwise you may be missing some very important pieces of information coming from it.

When my granddaughter, Lexi, was very young, I didn't see her for a few years as her mom and her dad, who is my son, are separated. When Lexi came back into our lives, I was blessed to be working with the animal spirit guides. I mentioned that she had a tiger with her and that one of the traits of the tiger is the ability to predict the future. When her mom heard this, she excitedly reported that when Lexi was very small, she had an *imaginary* tiger she talked to.

It is very interesting that what we, as adults, perceive to be fantasy is, in fact, very real. Although my granddaughter is now in her teens and her interest in my work is not as prominent as it used to be, she is very insightful. A few years after I revealed her spirit guide to her, she asked me if she would always know what was going to transpire before it happened. She was very deep in thought just before she asked me that question, and although she didn't reveal any information to me, I felt she was contemplating an incident that had happened to her. Lexi's tiger guide still accompanies her and is waiting for a resurgence of interest from his protégé. In the meantime, he keeps very close and provides guidance to her through her dreams.

If you don't know your main spirit guide, the meditation in the upcoming *Establishing a Connection* chapter will help you connect with it. All it takes is for you to be very open and allow your totem to make itself known, ignoring any preconceived ideas about what will appear.

My main spirit animal is a raven—which at the time it first became known to me would not have been my choice because of the biased opinion I had about ravens. That opinion was based on not understanding their true nature. Once I began to acknowledge their authentic traits, I loved and accepted Raven as my totem.

It is because of this experience that I ask you to be open right away. Your spirit animal has already waited long enough for you to acknowledge it, without you overthinking its place in your life.

The poem, "Listen: Raven Speaks," at the beginning of this section, is my tribute to the raven and what it has guided me to. It was originally published in my first book, *Waves of Blue Light: Heal the Heart and Free the Soul,* in 2011. I included it here because the words still apply as Raven works with me to accomplish magic in my life. It is the magic of intention, accomplishment, personal growth, and spiritual enlightenment.

The raven is considered to be a friend of all animals, and it was Raven who encouraged me to quit eating meat when I was ready to release that need from my life. This amazing spirit helps me to connect with other animals, reuniting them with their human counterparts. The sagacity of Animal Spirit Guide Readings,[23] as a tool, furthers this connection as our energies merge into an unbeatable force as ancient as time itself. That is what your animal totem wants with you too.

As I am writing about the raven, I recall an incident that occurred a few years ago. My husband and I were coming out of Costco, heading toward our truck, when we noticed a raven sitting on top of the tailgate. Thinking it would fly away, we began putting groceries into the back seat. The raven just sat there—not moving. I decided to approach it, as we needed to put some heavier bags into the back of the truck. I began to walk toward it, speaking softly, thinking that at any moment it would fly away. It didn't take off as I had expected, but began moving to the far side of the tailgate, its claws making a clacking sound as it skittered farther away from me. So, I asked—as I always do—when there is an unusual physical altercation with an animal, "Do you have a message for me?" Upon asking this, the bird flew way.

There is one thing I remember the most: from the moment we approached the truck until the second he flew away, the raven didn't take his eyes off of me during the entire exchange.

Ravens are very prolific in the animal kingdom and are known for their wisdom and ability to transform consciousness. Interestingly, a group of ravens is known as an *unkindness*. However, Jordan, the writer of the following account, welcomed an enormous group of ravens, as their presence confirmed to her that she was on the right path.

---

23   Animal Spirit Guide Readings bring in the energies of the animals that have a message for you, as well as reveal your main totem.

A Raven Welcome

It was a moment that I will never forget …

I was really working hard on myself to grow spiritually, unconditionally love and accept myself, to forgive all others, and have peace in my life. I knew that I needed these results in order to be able to help others, as I feel that is my purpose in this life. I had also been communicating with and following the guidance of my angels and guides every day.

I knew that December 21, 2012, was going to be a powerful day, as prophecies revealed that it would be a spiritual time of awakening. We had a choice, and the 21st was the deadline to make the choice as to which way our life was going to go. I was not exactly sure what that meant, but took it to mean that a person will either spiritually improve their life or be stuck in the third dimension, holding on to things and dealing with third dimension emotions, making life difficult, and creating more havoc, anxiety, fear, and unhappiness. The 21st was coming up fast, and I had asked my guides if I was on the right path, as I was struggling in my life at the time.

One week before December 21, 2012, I was driving home from work on the same route that I had driven every day for the past seven years. It was along a back road on the south side of Saskatoon Mountain, Alberta—two miles away from where I live. On this stretch, there is nothing except open fields on either side of the road. As I was driving, I noticed a lot of black up in the trees ahead on both sides of the road. The trees hung over the road a bit, and that was also black—making it look like a tunnel. When I got closer, I realized that the black I saw in the trees came from ravens—hundreds of them! I was in complete awe as I had never, ever seen a raven at this spot before and definitely never that many in one place!

They were sitting perfectly placed in the trees, making it look like solid black around an opening that I was going to drive through, like a gateway, and it looked as if they were waiting for me. Weirdly enough, as I drew closer, none of them moved. It wasn't until I drove past them, through their gateway, that they took flight.

It was fascinating! The message that I received from this incident is that, spiritually, I was entering the next phase of my life. I had made it through the gateway and was going to be okay! It was exciting, and I alone was the one to experience this.

As soon as I saw the ravens, I knew it was a sign, because I had known for a while that my animal spirit guide is a raven. It made me feel incredible! I realized that it was a spiritual doorway I had gone through, by the shape of the opening and how the birds waited for me to pass through the arch before flying off. I knew then that I had made it, and I was on the right path!

—**Jordan Pomeroy** *is a mother of three young children who enjoys nature, animals, gardening, working with energy, and people.*

Our totems show up when we need them and usually reflect our own characteristics back to us.

The porcupines in this next story seem relentless, and as you read this narrative, you will understand why.

GOING FOR GOLD

My husband has a very firm belief in his ability to find that elusive gold nugget. He has been prospecting for gold for about six years now. He has staked claims and is very determined that he *will* find gold where he has staked.

At our mine site, we have had seven different encounters with porcupines. They have decided that our cabin is a good place to rub up against at night, and they love to chew on the plywood that makes up the outside of the cabin as well as the outhouse. We have had to pull quills out of our faithful watchdog three times.

My husband feels these porcupines are a plague. I know there is a different meaning for these encounters. My spirit guide book[24] notes the porcupine qualities include: *an appreciation of creation and a love of discovery, in a childlike manner. They are full of fantasy and imagination, and they honor the wonder of life. They are a joy-sharer and a gentle, good natured, nonaggressive, playful lover. They have faith and trust in the universe, along with a genuine humility and ease of embarrassment.*

Recently, my husband has learned how to dowse for gold. It is almost the same as witching for water; special rods are bent in an L-shape and placed in each one of the dowser's hands. The dowser then walks forward. When the rods cross, it is an indication of the location of a gold vein. My husband has an unfailing belief in this system, and it is a joy to see his faith shine through.

He has decided to retire and only work on his mining during the summer. Again, going back to my spirit guide book, it also states: "Balancing act, they are good at putting work and play together in a well-balanced diet. They know how to deal with the difficulties and to deflect the barbs of others while keeping the sense of wonder of the inner child strong. They mix having fun and exploring their curiosity with meeting the needs and achieving."

I have watched others catch my husband's faith and wait in anticipation for him to find gold. I have also heard others scoff at his ideas. He takes both of these views good-naturedly.

I am sure you are wondering about the success of finding gold. Well, each year, he finds a little more than the year before, and each year it is

---

[24] Animal Activities: Their Psycho-Symbolic Meanings—A Shaman's Guidebook—Narayan Singh

almost enough to pay for the expenses of operating the equipment that is needed to prospect. At the end of every season he says, "I know where it is now, and next year we will find it for sure!"

Can you see the *childlike appreciation for discovery as well as faith and trust in the universe?* I sure can, so I believe it is fitting that he is plagued with porcupines.

—Loretta Zaluski

ANIMAL GROUPINGS

Affirmation: In recognizing the importance of all species, I am open to benefiting from the limitless energy of all.

Connecting

For balance we strive
In all things,
Opening up to give and receive.

But yet, it seems
We condemn
What we don't understand.

It's easy to love
When we trust
And all goes well.

In misunderstanding,
We abuse
The misunderstood.

Not accepting
What all have to give
Creates a barrier.

Open up to agreement
And acknowledge
The gifts,

Making no mistake
Of the importance
Residing within

Not only of yourself,
But inside the heart
Of every living thing.

When identifying an animal's characteristics, grouping it into a category makes it easier for you to understand its underlying message for you. I have written about most of these groups throughout the book, but there are a couple that were missed mainly because I didn't have any stories about them to illustrate their importance.

One of these is the reptiles. I have a reptile—a snake named Adam. Adam is a ball python, and he is the gentlest creature I have ever handled. Adam came to me via my son, who bought him about fifteen years ago. There was once an Eve, as well, but, unfortunately, she passed a few years ago.

At one time I was afraid of snakes, but Adam and Eve changed all that for me. It is interesting to note that reptiles, snakes especially, are associated with healing (releasing the old and embracing the new). This is because they are able to shed their old skin and regrow a new one. I can definitely associate a fear of snakes to a fear of healing. It has only been in the last ten years that I have learned to let go and allow myself to heal physically, emotionally, mentally, and spiritually.

Reptiles, in general, are about transformation, so when they are around, you are about to go through some changes. I have a great friend who came to visit me (well—Adam really) last winter. She has been going through many shifts and is determined to release her fears. One of these fears is of snakes.

After spending an hour or so in Adam's company—holding him, petting him, and letting him coil around her—she fell in love with him. What a great testament in honoring your own healing! Sometimes all it takes is understanding your fears and meeting them.

Another group that was neglected is that of the mystical—those wonderful creatures of myth that capture our childhood and inner child imaginations. The dragons, unicorns, and centaurs, etc. show us how to embrace life's magic. Wherever they appear, expect mystery and intrigue to guide you.

The fish and all aquatic life remind us that we have the perseverance and adaptability to accomplish whatever we set our minds to. (Remember the seal story?)

The other groups are well covered:

We have the predators such as: the bear, coyote, ravens, and hawks. They show up when our lesson is about accomplishing goals or restoring natural balance.

The prey animals (some of which are also predators) such as cats, squirrels, and mice teach us about death, rebirth, and balance throughout the life cycle.

Birds help us to connect our conscious and unconscious minds and show us how much more we can be.

The insects whisper to us of our connection and ability to contribute within our communities and universally.

Each of these groups is essential to us, not only as a part of our physical world, but as a reminder to us of how valuable each one of us is. The world truly would not be the same if any one of these groups were absent.

ESTABLISHING A
CONNECTION

Affirmation: Connecting with my totem gives me insight and understanding into my life and how I create and respond to my experiences.

WHY CONNECT?

Connecting with your spirit animals gives you the opportunity to get to know your animal totem and guides so they can assist you in recognizing the strengths you possess and help you overcome your weaknesses.

As previously mentioned, your totem or power animal is one whose energy closely resembles that of your own. It is with you to offer you guidance along your path, helping you overcome obstacles by using the gifts you have. For example, my raven totem tells me that magic is all around me and also that I always know what to do in any situation. This reminder comes to me in the form of the raven when I am facing a tough decision or experiencing doubtful times. I will hear the raven call, or it will show up overhead when I am outside, or even fly right in front of my car when I am driving. Its presence reminds me of my capabilities to overcome any obstacles.

Once you are aware of your power animal, it will find unique ways to show itself to you in order to give you guidance in your life. It is a good idea to have a replica of your power animal somewhere where you can see it often as a reminder. I had a plate painting done of a raven, and it hangs right in my office. I often forget it is there, but when the occasion warrants it, my eyes seem to glance right at it.

Animal spirit guides, which are not necessarily your main totem, are those animals that show up in unusual ways to give you a message. They, too, are here to guide you in your daily life. Although any animal can be your spirit guide, you may find that there are certain ones that you see or feel more than others. These may be your secondary helpers, which also carry similar personality traits to you. I recognize the deer and the grouse or prairie chicken as mine. They are not as close to my energy as the raven, but they appear quite often to remind me they are here to help as well. The prairie chicken always prompts me to be myself regardless of the circumstances, and the deer tells me that grace and ease are called for in a situation. I can be quite intense sometimes, so these reminders are always very timely.

Many of you may be asking how to find your power animal and animal spirit guides. The next few pages are a meditation that will channel an answer to you.

IDENTIFYING YOUR ANIMAL SPIRIT GUIDES

Close your eyes and let your mind go blank. Take a couple of deep breaths and on the third breath, see yourself being transported on your out breath as you hear the whoosh of air leave your body. Feel the wind as it carries you along, above the tree tops—going higher and higher—until you can no longer see ground beneath you.

You are traveling to your higher consciousness, which is objective, and has no preconceived ideas about what you will find along the way to meeting your animal guides. This consciousness sees all forms of life as one unit, connecting each onto the other.

As you are being whisked along, the excitement of your journey deepens as your energy vibration increases the closer you get to your destination. The high vibration of the animal kingdom reaches out to you, and you feel a stronger and stronger pull. The wind seems to intensify, and you find yourself spiraling gently downward like a falling leaf.

As you descend, you arrive on an island that has every species of bird on it that has ever existed. Softly landing, you walk among the birds and soon spot a beach with sparkling white sand that you walk toward. You feel the warm sun beaming down on you, creating a shimmering mist. Walking through this mist, you find yourself on the other side of it and see before you every land animal that has ever lived. They are all minding their own business and don't even seem to notice that you are among them. Continuing on, you spot a vibrant blue color ahead of you and realize it is the ocean. The hot sun beating down pushes you toward the anticipated coolness of the water. Reaching the water's edge you walk into it, feeling the heat recede as you plunge your entire body into its depths.

Opening your eyes underwater, you see flashes of intermittent color and recognize that you have reached the home of every animal that has ever dwelled in water. There are fish, whales, dolphins, and water creatures of myth. You stay there for a while, fascinated by their close proximity and seeming unaffectedness of your presence. Once you have had your fill of this mesmerizing sight, you swim toward an underwater cave you see to your right. You are curious but unafraid of what you will find within this cave.

You reach the cave entrance and are riveted by what you see before you. It is like a heavenly garden. Bees are buzzing around flowers while dragonflies and butterflies are flitting everywhere. There are spiders weaving in the corners and ants crawling over your toes. You recognize some of the insects in this paradise, although not all of them, and realize that what you are witnessing is a kind of insect heaven. The perfume fragrance of the flowers and their vivid rainbow colors entice you into moving farther into this blissful, peaceful haven.

As you move around their habitat, the insects ignore you and even seem to move out of your way as you make your way back to the cave entrance. Looking around you once more, you are pleasantly surprised when you feel yourself being wrapped up in silken thread.

The thread acts as a net, and you feel yourself being lifted up—gently and slowly. As you rise, you have a sense of excitement in wondering what will happen next. You don't have to wait too long to find out, as before you know it, you feel the net opening to transfer you to a platform high above a dimly lit area with reptiles of all kinds—all that have ever been known to man—lounging below. You realize that you are not frightened but awed at the strength and beauty of these magnificent creatures. You gaze at them for a while as they carry on with their business, seemingly unaware of your presence.

You feel the platform beginning to rise and soon find yourself in a mystical environment full of color and vibrant energy. You realize that you have entered the land of possibilities. All those amazing worlds you explored as a child, from the unicorn to the dragon, reside here. This world of imagination is alive with every mythical creature you have ever heard or dreamed of. Your inner child would love to stay and play, but you realize how long you have already been gone and hold this place in your heart for another day.

As you get ready to leave, one of the most beautiful presences you have ever encountered approaches you and gently blows out its sweet breath. You find yourself gently riding on this breath, just enjoying the floating sensation, when you suddenly become aware of energy around you. Looking about, you see a few members of the animal kingdom riding with you on this beautiful wave. Sitting beside you, you see your power or totem animal and behind you are your animal spirit guides—all having followed you out of their habitats.

Their presence is comforting, and you know that when you open your eyes, as you come back into your physical body, they will be right there, helping you, guiding you, and reminding you of the strengths you have and the promise of knowledge yet to come.

How do you feel about your totem and guides? Are you surprised by what they are?

You can use several different resources to interpret the energy meanings of these powerful helpers. Any of the books I have listed in the beginning introduction will give you an accurate energy meaning, or you can go online, or access any other material you may have about animal meanings.

My animal totem is:

Its characteristics include:

I share the following traits with my totem:

My totem has these traits that I do not see within myself yet, but as a potential for me:

I recognize these traits as those I no longer carry:

My secondary totems include:

1.

2.

3.

4.

Their characteristics are:

1.

2.

3.

4.

They are helping me with:

1.

2.

3.

4.

Notes:

NOTES

YOUR QUESTIONS
ANSWERED

Affirmation: Questioning and being open to the answers elevates my body, mind, and soul to a new level of awareness.

I am often asked questions about our animal friends and so include many of those questions and answers here to help clarify any uncertainties about working with animal guides and totems.

Can animals reincarnate into other animals?

Animals are an energy, just as we are, and one thing we know is that energy can never die, so it has to go somewhere. Why couldn't it reemerge into the physical characteristics of another animal? The soul may choose to be reborn into another form of life or into the same genus it recently vacated. It all depends on the lessons it chooses to learn in its new lifetime.

Can we (humans) be reincarnated into animals?

The human soul can be transported into the form of an animal. Some of the stories you read in this book tell about loved ones coming back in the form of a bird in order to let their family know they are okay. As animals generally do not have as long a physical life as humans do, it again depends on the experiences the soul wants to have. The soul may need only a short time to complete lessons, and those lessons may be best accomplished in animal form.

One afternoon when my granddaughter was about four or five years old, she was totally engrossed in thought while we were taking a walk through the woods on our property. When she let out a big sigh, I asked her what she was thinking about. She completely took me by surprise when she said, "I just don't know what I want to be." I remember telling her that she had many years to consider her future and that it wasn't something she had to worry about right now.

"But, Grandma," she replied. "How do you decide? There are so many things to be. I could be a bird or a dog or a horse, or even a fish, in my next life."

How exciting to be completely open to so many possibilities! We can learn so much about life from children as well as animals.

What does it mean when I see a dead animal on the side of the road or hit one myself?

It is an indicator of the energy of that specific animal prompting you to use caution, within that particular energy. It is also a reminder about the frailty of life, alerting you to the benefits of slowing down to experience life rather than hurry through each day.

When you actually hit an animal with your vehicle, you are being given a very specific cue about how you are using your time here. Are you being too careless or too cautious? Are your boundaries nonexistent?

Study the characteristics of the animals you come into contact with for more insight into their individual energy and reflect on how that applies to your life.

Also, please say a blessing to help the animal's spirit on its way anytime you notice a lifeless carcass.

I have a fear of certain animals; is there a meaning behind that?

It could be that you had an experience with that particular animal that instilled a belief about it (such as getting bitten by a dog—so now you avoid them). It could also be a belief created by media, such as television, movies, or even a news item about an event that happened to someone else, and you have accepted it as a truth for yourself.

As animal species have different energy characteristics associated with them, they relate to us as individuals, so we can learn from them. Just because one person had an experience with a bear doesn't mean that you will have the same incident happen to you. The bear confrontation is meant to be meaningful to the individual who encountered it.

If you have an unfounded fear of a certain animal, study its characteristics. It is not the animal itself that you are afraid of, but the meaning of its energy.

For example, two common fears are mice and snakes. Studying mouse energy, you can see that the mouse is a victim being pursued as food by many other animals. Do you see yourself as a victim? Mice are also known as being caught up in details. Are you too immersed in details and trying to get everything just right instead of allowing the unexpected? What scares you about that?

Snakes are healing energy. They shed their skin regularly, allowing growth and change. Do you fear change? These are just a couple of examples.

I am not saying you should go out of your way to approach an animal you fear, but it doesn't benefit you to bow to superstition either.

Will I always have the same animal totem?

Since your totem animal carries aspects of your personality, it is possible that the same animal will accompany you for a lifetime. Having stated that, though, if you change drastically in your life, your power animal may change as well. Your secondary guides are more likely to change if their reminders become second nature to you. In that case, you will no longer need their guidance, as you already recognize it within you. Your totem animal is so close to your own traits that it is least likely to be replaced once you reach adulthood, but not impossible.

As a child, you are still forming your personality, so your totem is more likely to change during the years of zero to eight and then become permanent after that.

Is your power animal an animal that you are the most attracted to?

Not at all. Since I began working with animal totems, I have come upon some animal species I am not familiar with and, often, neither are the people who have that animal as a totem. What is important is that it resonate with you in some way. Even though I had never been particularly fond of the raven before I knew it as my totem, the idea of it as my power animal really intrigued me—especially after I learned its traits.

What if I don't feel a connection with my spirit animal or animal totem once I have identified them?

They could be new to you as you may have recently moved into another level of perception, so their energy may not resonate with yours yet. Research their traits and get to know them. You may be working with preconceived ideas of the animal that creates a barrier with them. As you get to know them better, notice the potential that they are bringing to you and the energetic qualities they work with. These are probably the traits that are developing within you, which you have yet to recognize.

I have been told that I have a different animal totem with me by different people. How do I know what to believe?

I suggest that you find out what each animal represents energetically, then see which of them have traits that are closely related to yours and what resonates with you the most. I caution you to look beyond what you perceive to be the *stars* of the animal kingdom to the often hidden traits of those animals that are thought of as less desirable. You never know what you will find. Working through the meditation in this book can also help you determine which animals are with you.

My animal totem is a giraffe. How is it possible for me to receive messages from a giraffe when they don't live nearby?

Good question! Your totem will get a message to you in other ways besides appearing physically in front of you. Be aware of the times you see the giraffe on TV, in a card reading, in a picture, as an ornament, etc.—especially if these sightings are one after the other or all occur within a few days. If you know what your totem signifies energetically, these sightings will remind you of those qualities. I know people who have collected representations of certain animals, just because they like that animal, and then find out that their collection is of their totem!

You have been receiving messages all along without being aware of it; awareness will be your guide.

What does it mean when I find abandoned birds' nests—sometimes with eggs in them and sometimes with no eggs?

If you find a nest without eggs in it, it means that you have reached a point on your journey where you can *leave the nest and fly on your own*. What has been happening in your life lately that you are unwilling to let go of? You are ready to move on—know that you will be supported in your choice to do so.

A nest with abandoned eggs indicates reluctance on your part to move forward in some area. Are you feeling a lack of support in your life somewhere? Are you feeling abandoned by the universe and at the mercy of unknown forces? Examine your early years to see where this sense of aloneness may have come from; release whatever is holding you back from reaching your highest potential. Also, determine what type of animal formerly occupied the nest to get more specific information as to what is happening in your own life.

As I write this, I am reminded of a robin's nest with three eggs in it that I spotted just the other day (unusual for the end of July). I really had to chuckle as I have been rewriting and reviewing this manuscript for months now. I was being given the message that it is time to let this book go—it has been sitting on my computer (nest) for long enough—now is the perfect time for it to be born.

Keeping an eye on the nest during the next few days, after I noticed it hidden in my raspberry bushes, I saw each new baby bird as it emerged, reminding me of the projects I have been carefully incubating and watching come to life, individually and each in their own time. As a robin sighting means *new beginnings*, I realize it is time to welcome new experiences.

Does everyone have an animal guide or totem?

Yes, everyone has spirit helpers in one form or another. Most of us don't recognize them as being with us. Although they are not in a physical body, their energetic traits identify them as one species or another. We, humans, are inclined to label almost everything, so we tend to perceive our helpers as if they were in physical form.

Everything is an aspect of ourselves.

REFERENCES

Books

Andrews, Ted. *Animal Speak: The Spiritual and Magical Powers of Creatures Great and Small.* Llewellyn Publications; 1993

Farmer, Steven. D. *Animal Spirit Guides.* California: Hay House, Inc.; 2006

Singh, Narayan. *Animal Activities: A Shaman's Handbook: Their Psychosymbolic Meanings;* Lynn Henderson Publications, 2003

Websites

http://www.psychicsuniverse.com/articles/spirituality/ living-spiritual-life/spiritual-power-humble-bee

http://wiki.answers.com/Q/Spiritual meaning of grasshoppers#slide=1

http://www.whats-your-sign.com/grasshopper-totem-and-symbolism.html

ACKNOWLEDGEMENTS

Story Authors

Thank you to the very special people below who have allowed your stories to be published in this book. My vision for this work would not have been realized without your very generous contributions. Thank you for the time you spent putting your amazing tales together and giving all of us the benefit of your wisdom and apparent love of all creatures. I am so glad to have gotten to know you better through your stories and our communication back and forth during the writing of this book. This work is dedicated to all of you. It has been an amazing year of connections, and I am blessed to know each and every one of you!

Catherine Courtine
Carrie Currie
Helaine (Lanie) Dufoe
Cheryl Frank
Helene Gamache
Debbi J. Helm
Tania Hicks
Bonnie Ireland
Dale Kardas
Denise Kendall
Keith Lyons
Elisa Marie
Julia Oh
Christina Otterstrom-Cedar
Jordan Pomeroy
Arinder Sanun
Don Shine (White Raven)
Pearl Smith
Owen Stanford

Jeanette Taylor-Mac
Loretta Zaluski

Image Authors

Svetlana Alyuk
Elenarts
Jill Erin
Johannes Gerhardus Swanepoel
Eric Isselee
Katkov
Viktoria Makarova
Andrey Pavlov
Michael Pettigrew
Ulga
Destiny VisPro

Index

CPSIA information can be obtained at www.ICGtesting.com
Printed in the USA
LVOW11s0724100315

429833LV00002B/131/P